WHEN GROUPS COME TOGETHER, GREAT THINGS HAPPEN

Internal MASTERMINDS

How Smart Talent Leaders Create Engagement and Pivot Organizational Culture

Sylvia Henderson
InternalMASTERMINDS.com

Sylvia Henderson • Josh Silverstone

V-TWIN PRESS

Title/Subtitle: **INTERNAL MASTERMINDS: How Smart Talent Leaders Create Engagement and Pivot Organizational Culture**

Author(s): Sylvia Henderson and Josh Silverstone
Publisher: V-Twin Press
Cover design and book layout: Carolyn Sheltraw
Printed in the United States of America
Editor: Erin Nunnally

To order this title, please contact MindTeam Solutions, Inc. Up-to-date contact information is at www.MindTeamSolutions.com.

Library of Congress Cataloging-in-Publication Data

Henderson, Sylvia.
Silverstone, Josh.
INTERNAL MASTERMINDS: How Smart Talent Leaders Create Engagement and Pivot Organizational Culture / by Sylvia Henderson and Josh Silverstone
p. cm.
Includes images, bibliographical references, quotations, notes, additional resources web links
ISBN 978-1-932197-50-1 (paperback)

1. Business. 2. Organizational Development. 3. Leadership Development.

We dedicate this book first and foremost to the people who are closest to our hearts, sacrifice for and support our successes, and lift us up when we encounter our lessons from which we learn: our partners and family.

Pat

Jenn

Vivian

Griff

And to our friends, advisors, and supporters without whom our business, this book, and our sanity would not be possible. (Okay…two out of three, anyway!)

Alan,
Thanks so much for joining us in the studio. Love your energy & stories. Looking forward to future conversations & collaboration.
Best,
Josh

Table of Contents

Foreword
By Mark LeBlanc

Never before have people been asked to do so much in so little time and with so few resources. Sylvia and Josh have created a blueprint for you, as a corporate leader, to get a handle on creativity and innovation. We often look to outside experts for the answers when the cumulative wisdom you are looking for may be right under your nose.

Are you tapping into the ideas and insights from the people who have a pulse on what is going on in your organization? The strategy of assembling inner circles or internal masterminds within your ranks can reveal answers in real time.

The value of dialogue is often underestimated and underappreciated. In order to outthink and outsmart your competition, it is critical that you create an environment where peoples' knowledge and genius are heard and harnessed. In this book, Josh and Sylvia provide you with what you need to know and what you need to do in order to create a shift in thinking.

When people are given an opportunity to provide perspective in a safe and supportive environment, it creates an idea think tank. Never underestimate the value of one idea that can change a culture or move mountains in the marketplace. All too often, good ideas are dismissed and great ideas are never even heard.

No change. No change.

You have nothing to lose and everything to gain by creating internal masterminds that can shine a light on the best ideas for productivity and performance. As someone who has benefitted personally by being in a mastermind group for nearly thirty years, I can attest to the power of the collaborative spirit.

Every organization, large or small, would do well to use this book as a lighthouse guide. Having Sylvia and Josh on your team will make the ultimate difference in turning vision into reality.

Mark

Mark LeBlanc, CSP

Speaker, Business Coach and Author of *Never Be the Same, Build Your Consulting Practice* and *Growing Your Business!*

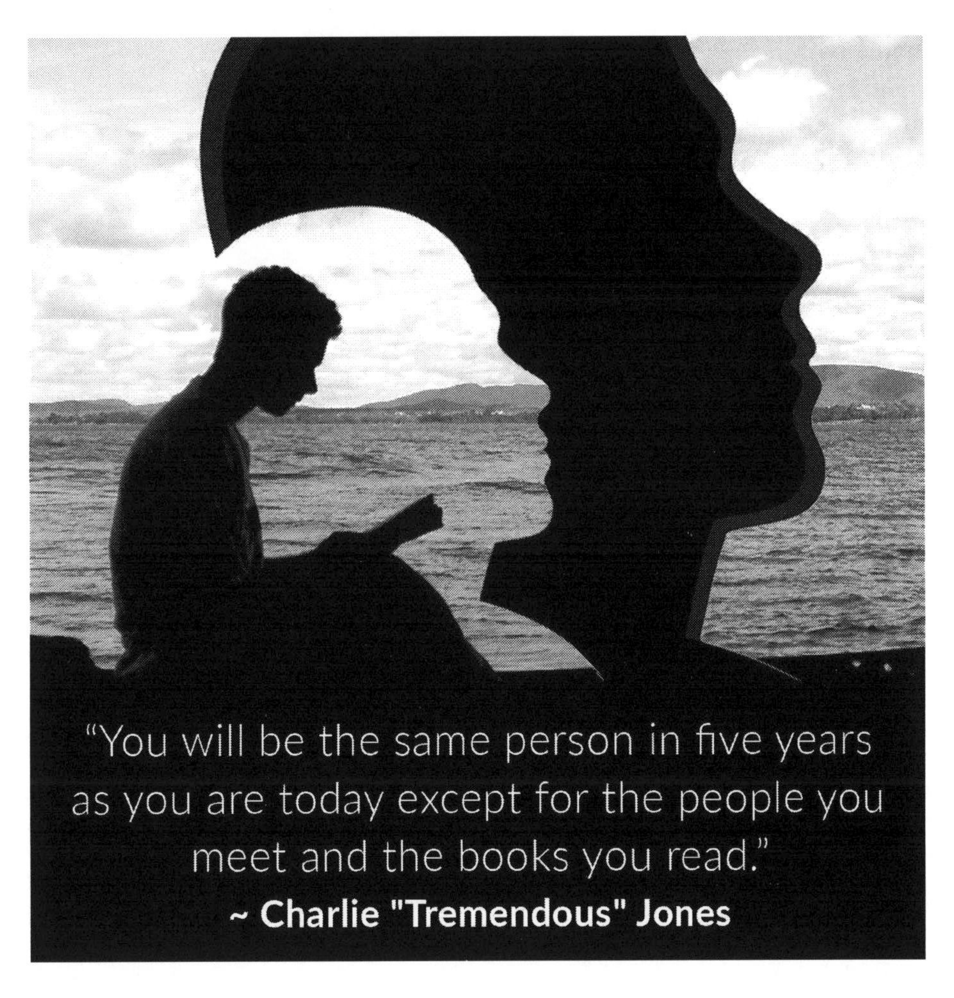

"You will be the same person in five years
as you are today except for the people you
meet and the books you read."
~ Charlie "Tremendous" Jones

"Transformation literally means going beyond your form."
~ Wayne Dyer

"Here's to the crazy ones. The misfits. The rebels. The troublemakers. The round pegs in the square holes. The ones who see things differently. And while some may see them as the crazy ones, we see genius. Because the people who are crazy enough to think they can change the world, are the ones who do."
~ Rob Siltanen

Introduction

Let's just get this out at the beginning.
Who ever heard of a business book that opens this way, in landscape profile?
And why would we risk your acceptance by doing this?

Our response: Who says books have to be formatted the "normal way" of a typical business book layout?

Because it's the way it has always been done?

Since our message is about pivoting and taking a different approach to organizational culture and employee engagement, we thought that a book representing such a shift was appropriate.

Pivoting, a new way of thinking, or changing your perspective, causes you to think differently. We want you to consider a perspective that differs from the status quo. Our messaging is about implementing an approach to your organization's culture, internal communications, employee engagement and retention, and idea acceptance and implementation to grow your business, achieve your desired outcomes, be more agile, and thrive.

One of us authors enjoys solving puzzles, and the other enjoys winning at poker. Sylvia's favorite puzzles are picture puzzles – finding the differences between two seemingly-identical photos, finding hidden drawings inside larger drawings, and jigsaw puzzles. When she gets stuck solving the first two of these while holding them upright, she turns the page or mobile screen 90°, then 180°, and then 270° to give her different perspectives. When she gets stuck with a jigsaw puzzle, she scatters the pieces in different orders for the same reason. Changing perspectives may not solve the puzzles completely, yet the process accelerates her progress. Even when she returns the puzzles to their upright positions, she cannot see the original problem the same way again.

Apply these puzzle problem-solving strategies to your employees and culture. When you change your perspective, you see your environment differently and can take actions that better lead to achieving your desired outcomes.

As for Josh, he plays poker not just to make certain winning hands. He assesses the opponent and situation, calculates the odds, and executes a quick decision. By understanding people and knowing basic math and statistics, he is able to put himself in winning positions. He uses this information to take confident actions and feel good about his choices regardless of individual outcomes.

Leaders and organizations can learn a lot from the idea of having a process to evaluate information, make decisions, and take action. This requires setting goals and taking risks to do something differently than you've previously done.

Trending with business books are creative authors who distinguish themselves by writing books that read both from the front and from the back. Therefore, that format is no longer unique in the publishing ecosystem.

Many children's books are designed to a landscaped layout – wider than higher. Since we're writing about how to pivot – or even transform – organizational culture and improve bottom line results through your people, we decided to model pivoting and transformation by pivoting this business book layout.

The Merriam Webster dictionary defines "disruption" as a disturbance or problem that interrupts an event, activity, or process; to interrupt the normal course or unity thereof. We add to this disrupting the "way-it's-always-been" mindset.

"Pivoting" is a familiar concept in the business startup world. When a founder's first business model does not work as planned (and this happens more often than not), the CEO, Board, and leadership team pivot to "Plan B"...and sometimes "Plan C" and beyond.

"Transformation" is defined as "a thorough or dramatic change in form or appearance; a metamorphosis".

From our perspective as consultants, educators, organizational development professionals and business owners, one must disrupt the status quo in order to transform thinking, behaviors, environments, and society. Transformation is about being innovative; in front of the curve; an influencer; creative; setting trends. For us, pivoting is trying something different with our book approach. Why not practice what we believe and write about by *doing* transformation?

Thus, you are now holding a book pivoted, disrupted, and transformed.

If this is an uncomfortable reality for you, ask yourself, "Why?"

Is discomfort with something new and different a pattern in the rest of your life or in your business? Is it initially inconvenient until you figure out how to adjust, adapt, and see it as an opportunity?

Are you open-minded enough to continue reading to discover a concept and practice that you can implement to transform the outcomes you realize in your business, profession, practice, or organization?

On these pages we write about a concept, platform, and process that you can apply to your organization and put into immediate action. Your mindset towards what you read here determines whether you stay with us through the entire book, consider what you discover, and then do what you determine you need to do to move from thoughts to organizational transformation.

Enough explaining disruption and transformation. Let's get to discovering what these internal masterminds are, their value to you and your organization, and how you can apply and implement them to engage employees, solidify or pivot culture, and transform your organization so that it thrives.

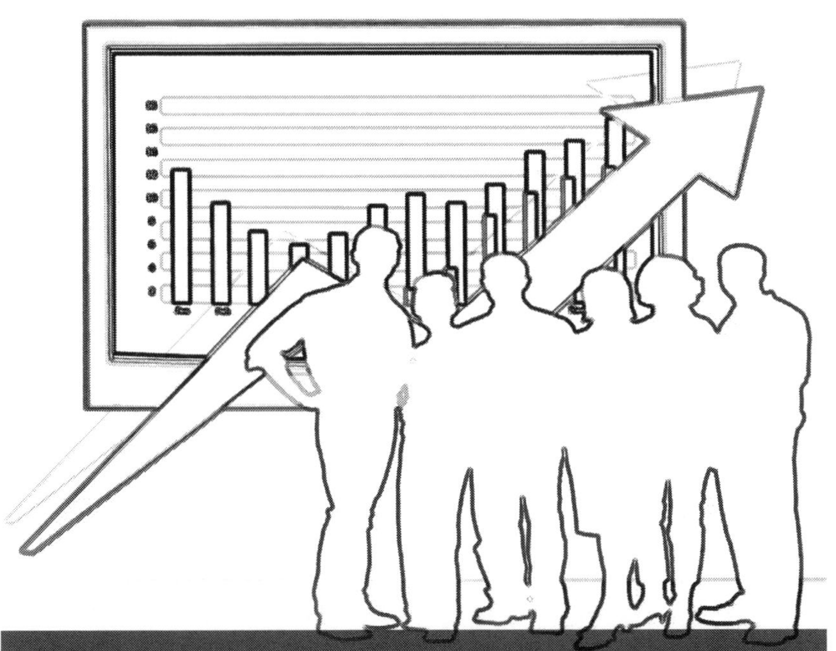

"Growth is seldom by mere chance. It is the result of forces working together."

~ James Cash Penney, Retail Magnate

"I define connection as the energy that exists between people when they feel seen, heard, and valued; when they can give and receive without judgment; and when they derive sustenance and strength from the relationship."

~ Brené Brown

"It really boils down to this: that all life is interrelated. We are all caught in an inescapable network of mutuality, tied into a single garment of destiny. Whatever affects one destiny, affects all indirectly."

~ Martin Luther King, Jr.

"You are the average of the five people with whom you spend the most time."

~Jim Rohn

Chapter 1
In Pursuit of Connection

These words represent our ultimate pursuit – connection and significance.

We seek social media groups; meet-ups; networks; advisory boards; masterminds; retreats; conferences; roundtables and the like as vehicles for personal, business, and cause-related connection. Ironically the more time we spend online, in front of screens, or with virtual-reality technology, the more we seek in-person, face-to-face connection.[1]

Consider the following words and their impact as they relate to your organization:

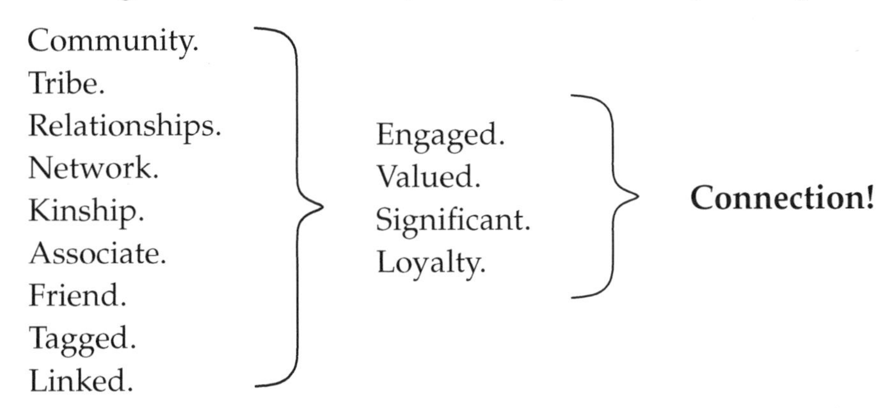

- ✓ Productivity improves by 20-25% in organizations with connected employees. (Source: The McKinsey Global Institute)

- ✓ Organizations with highly engaged employees have an average 3-year revenue growth 2.3 times greater than companies whose employees are only engaged at an average level. (Source: UNC Kenanflager Business School)

- ✓ Increasing employee engagement investments by 10% can increase profits by $2,400 per employee per year.
(Source: Workplace Research Foundation)

- ✓ Actively disengaged employees cost the U.S. $450 to $550 billion per year in lost productivity (Source: Gallup State of U.S. Workplace)

Employees go from employer to employer – and sometimes out on their own as entrepreneurs – in part to achieve connection and make a difference. Six in ten Millennials — the USA's largest generation, born between 1981-1996 — say they are looking for new employment opportunities. The cost of turnover is estimated at $30 billion annually. (Source: Gallup)

Entrepreneurs often work alone. Even so, they have ideas and need to bounce them off of others for different perspectives. They need trust, similar values, support, loving honesty, and no judgement when they share their ideas openly.

Engaged employees show initiative, make decisions, take risks, understand the organization's mission and leaders' vision, and know where and how they fit into the picture with their contributions in order to get ahead.

Leaders need to let go and let their people contribute, make mistakes, learn, grow, and feel respected in order for both people and company to thrive.

People form groups to fulfill their connection needs, yet few groups last long-term.

Peer Group Challenges

Common reasons why peer groups are typically short-lived experiences:

- Lack systems and processes.
- Little or zero leadership.
- Poorly-skilled leadership.
- Too many people in the group.
- Individuals lack spotlight opportunities.
- Too little participation.
- Lack of commitment.
- Little or zero follow-up and accountability.
- Lack of group purpose.
- Irregular or uncertain meetings.
- Poor meeting time management.
- Members receive little value for themselves.
- High-level organizational support lacking.
- Interruptions allowed during meetings.
- Environment unwelcoming.
- Members feel unsafe.
- Judgement rather than supportive input.

Why?

We authors studied groups of business people, professionals, executives, founders, entrepreneurs, and practitioners. These are people with heavy resource demands and little time for wasted and unproductive meetings. We researched what works and does not work for group longevity.

We took what we learned and created a group platform that serves where others fall short. We now implement this group platform with entrepreneurs and within organizations. We've run successful groups over multiple years putting what we learned into action.

Generations of people more comfortable with online connections need processes, systems, specific tools and action steps to guide them in establishing and maintaining successful in-person and virtual groups. Group structure, processes, and a support system are pillars of the platform that we share with you in this book. We identify what does and does not work for establishing intentional, collaborative, productive, high-performing peer groups where the concept of the "third mind" is key to the need for and outcomes from such groups.

Use this book as a guide for creating your connection and engagement platform. If you wish to understand yet leave the "doing" to experts in the process, engage us at MindTeam Solutions, Inc. We will work with you to establish our group platform in your organization for your leaders and front-line staff.

[1] Sources:

- *Connecting People* Study. King's College. https://connectingpeoplestudy.net/home-page/
- *Connect to Thrive.* Psychology Today. https://www.psychologytoday.com/us/blog/feeling-it/201208/connect-thrive
- *Wired to Connect*. Scientific American. https://www.scientificamerican.com/article/why-we-are-wired-to-connect/?print=true
- State of U.S. Workplace: https://news.gallup.com/search/default.aspx?q=state+of+us+workplace+2018
- Workplace Research Foundation: https://talentculture.com/6-eye-opening-employee-engagement-statistics/
- UNC Kenanflager Business School: https://www.kenan-flagler.unc.edu/executive-development/about/~/media/E93A57C2D74F4E578A8B1012E70A56FD.ashx
- The McKinsey Global Institute: https://www.mckinsey.com/industries/high-tech/our-insights/the-social-economy

Journal

How do you seek business and professional connections?

With whom do you connect? In person? Online?

Who are your top five *close* connections with whom you interact for professional or business support?

Within your organization, how do you enable meaningful connections so your business thrives?

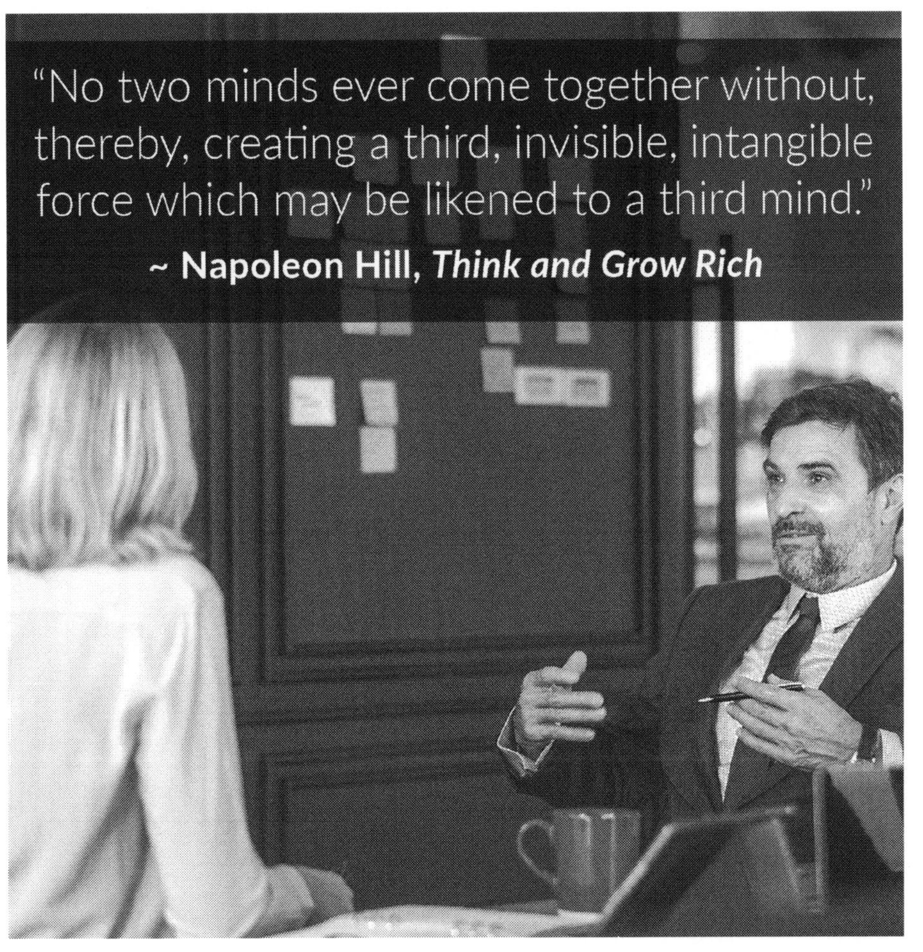

"No two minds ever come together without, thereby, creating a third, invisible, intangible force which may be likened to a third mind."
~ Napoleon Hill, *Think and Grow Rich*

"Many ideas grow better when transplanted into another mind than the one where they sprang up."
~ Oliver Wendell Holmes

"Great minds discuss ideas; average minds discuss events; small minds discuss people."
~ Eleanor Roosevelt

"We cannot solve our problems with the same thinking we used when we created them."
~ Albert Einstein

Chapter 2

Power of the "Third Mind"

Do you ever sit down with a friend or colleague and share an idea or ask a question about a challenge you're facing? Do you both talk it out to develop a solution, ending up with an approach, strategy, or revelation you doubt you would have thought of on your own?

Have you ever been so much in your own head about a situation that you couldn't see a way out that was right in front of you when someone else pointed it out?

These are examples of the concept of the third mind. A third mind manifests when two (or sometimes more) people identify solutions or bring clarity to situations as if a third person appeared outside of each of them separately. Together, the two create a third entity when they put their minds together. Thus the formula 1+1=3 represents the power of the third mind.

The third mind is more than one person sharing or talking with another. It is more than a one-to-one conversation. It is more than one person coaching or counseling or guiding another. It develops when there is a deeper interchange of ideas, thoughts, and questions-and-answers. After a back and forth exchange, an "a-ha!" moment happens. That a-ha moment is when the third mind is realized.

This is the concept of the third mind. Execution takes place when you create the environment that allows for establishing connections where people can experience the power of the third mind within your organization.

When people participate in intentional, collaborative groups where the core values of the group manifest the power of the third mind, group members feel connected and valued, ideas and solutions flow freely, and organizations grow, pivot, and thrive. These types of groups have a variety of designations such as inner circles, mastermind groups, advisory boards, and meet-ups.

Throughout the world, for people in different roles, professions, and niches, these groups endure as a testament to the fact that "when groups come together, great things happen"!

Additional suggested reading:

- *Think and Grow Rich – The Original 1937 Unedited Edition.* Napoleon Hill. Napoleon Hill Foundation. http://www.naphill.org/shop/books/think-and-grow-rich/

Journal

What is the *most recent* situation where you shared an idea with a colleague or confidante and realized your "a-ha" moment?

What was the value to you of the other person's perspective and insights? Did you avoid a mistake or save time, money, energy, or resources as a result?

Would you have come to the resulting conclusion or realization had you not had such an exchange of ideas?

How might you encourage such idea exchanges, efficiencies, or additional opportunities in your organization with your leaders or staff?

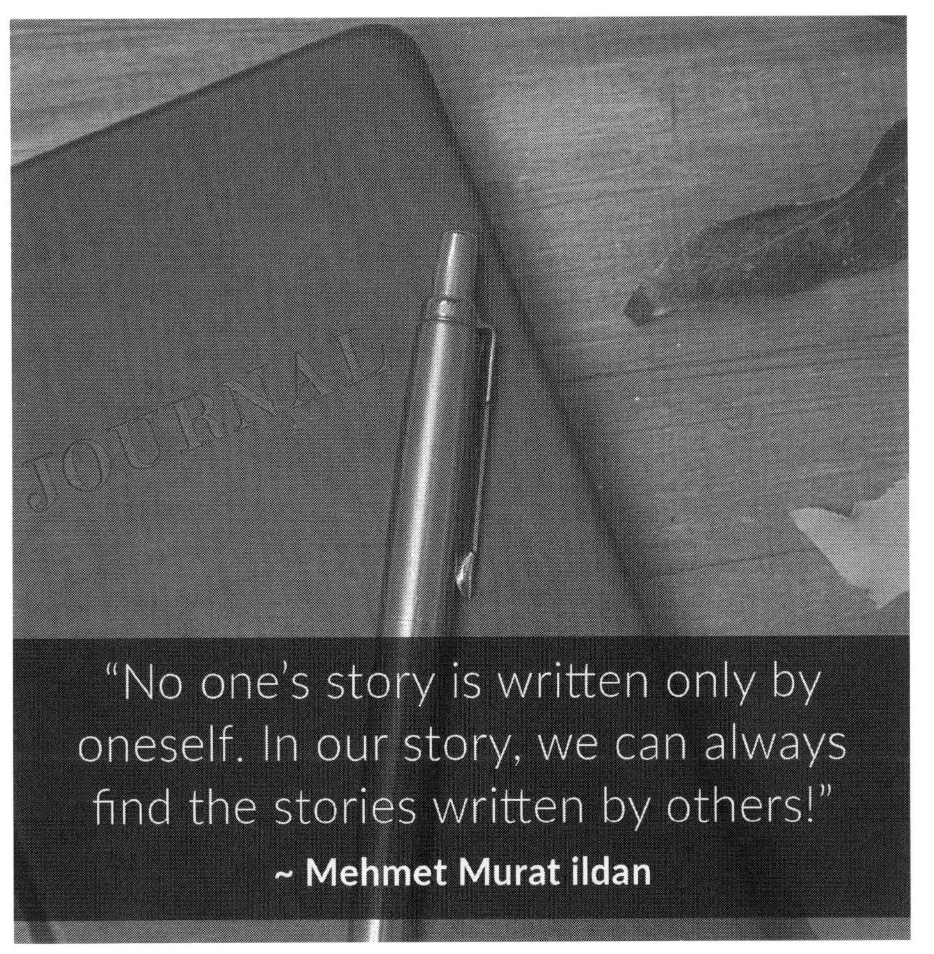

JOURNAL
"No one's story is written only by oneself. In our story, we can always find the stories written by others!"
~ Mehmet Murat ildan

"The significance - and ultimately the quality - of the work we do is determined by our understanding of the story in which we are taking part."

~ Wendell Berry

"Never doubt your story has value, and merit, and by sharing it you could help someone else you have never met come to terms with something in their life."

~ Holly Salsman

Chapter 3

Sharing Our Passion With You: Our Stories

To accept what we share with you and what may be a new concept to consider implementing, first discover what inspires us to do so. We share our stories with you hoping that you recognize some of your own and realize why we are passionate about you implementing and experiencing the power of the third mind.

Sylvia's Story

1975-1995. I worked for a Fortune 50 multi-national corporation, starting as a Customer Service Rep (CSR) front-line employee troubleshooting clients' computer hardware issues. I then moved to teaching other CSRs how to do the same as well as how to be their best professional selves. I continued climbing the corporate ladder, ending up as the Manager of Training and Development.

I left the company that had initially guaranteed employment until retirement after my division was sold to another company – twice. Corporate culture and employee benefits changed. Core values changed. The new work environment – as well as the business environment overall – was not in 1995 as it was in 1975.

The earlier company culture was such that I was taught, encouraged, and rewarded for ownership of my piece of the company. No, not through stock – although I acquired shares over the years. It was not the compensation – although I was paid well in salary, benefits, and small bonuses for exceeding performance goals. It was that from my first day on the job, although I was one of almost 400,000 employees, I was told that what I did mattered. I was responsible for treating my part of the company, my territory, as if it were my own business. I felt valued and respected, that I mattered in the scheme of the business. Although I was one of so many thousands of employees, I felt that my contributions were unique and meaningful.

Management reinforced my values by providing opportunities for me to contribute ideas and receive direct feedback as to whether my ideas were heard, and implemented.

The company slogans included words and phrases like, "RESPECT FOR THE INDIVIDUAL", "[Company Name] MEANS SERVICE", and "THINK". These words not only appeared throughout the company on posters and in written materials; they were also emphasized by management and built into our performance measures.

Was my twenty-year career with that company idyllic? Of course not. Did I experience biases and receive negative treatment from some of my colleagues for whatever reasons they deemed necessary for their own self-worth? Certainly. Yet overall, top-down practices and support of the company's core values made up for the individual behaviors and attitudes of a few insecure people.

As a manager of other people I then communicated the company culture to my employees and practiced the engagement, retention, and idea-encouraging behaviors with my staff.

The culture changed after we were acquired by two other companies. I witnessed and experienced the negative effects for my staff and myself. Engagement and loyalty decreased. Communication top-down and horizontally between departments lessened and in some cases ceased. Our benefit plans were reduced in value. People left, including myself after twenty years.

I vowed that, whether I led people at another company (I did) or started my own (I did, later), I would create a culture similar to that which I was fortunate enough to experience in the early, impressionable years of my corporate career. I committed to practice the engagement, retention, and idea empowerment behaviors for my employees that I learned were missing for so many of my friends, family, and contacts in other less-evolved companies and organizations.

This commitment is my passion driving me to help founders, owners, and leaders create loyalty, engagement, and ownership from the top executives down to the front-line staff that can lead them to achieve their desired outcomes, encourage innovation, increase profitability, and cause their organizations to thrive.

Through the ideas and guidance in this book, my business partner, co-author, and friend Josh and I introduce you to a solution with a structure and tools that enable you to create such an organization for yourself and your team.

Josh's Story

Sales is a language I've learned to become fluent in over the last two decades. Starting from the time I worked in retail during my teenage years, I quickly learned to help people get what they want and feel good about their decision. While working my way through college for a national retail chain, I received recognition as being ranked in the top 10% of sales associates in the country. Having achieved such a notable accomplishment so early into my job tenure, I began to realize that I may have a knack for sales which could become an exciting and fulfilling career in business.

After college I worked at a few different small and mid-sized businesses. In addition to selling, I became more skilled at wearing many hats, as required of employees and owners of smaller organizations. At my first job out of school, my sales efforts quickly came to include event planning and execution. Before I knew it I was a top producer, bringing in more than a quarter of the company's revenue. The long hours and the hard work were expected of my first job after college, and in my view, were paying off based on my sales success.

It was a few weeks later when the business owner publicly chastised me in front of my colleagues. Even looking back now, over a decade later, his comments were inappropriate to say the least. But what still gets me is how demoralizing the experience was and how quickly a hardworking, loyal, strong employee became unmotivated. I pretty swiftly identified that this was not the business culture I wanted to work in. I found the opportunity to make an upward career progression to outside sales at another company.

I found a good fit doing print advertising sales. At this company, I was the youngest sales employee. Within my first three months there I was awarded as the "employee of the quarter." Rapidly exceeding my sales goals, I was internally promoted to sales manager. Seeing the evolution of the media industry, I knew that print media was not where the long-term opportunities were for our market. At the time, the board did not want to move in the direction of online expansion, so upper management and the company had to make do.

Before I was recruited into sales management for the hospitality industry and left print advertising, I also saw the negative impact that a toxic employee was having on the culture and employees. This employee had one of the best territories but acted like she was untouchable. Instead of being humble or grateful, she acted like she was better than everyone else. She became increasingly rude, making fun of others, violating their personal space, and bullying those she felt threatened by. Although it's normal for management to be wary of dealing with a problematic employee who is responsible for a large chunk of revenue, action needed to be taken.

The executives above me had brought her into their office to speak with her from time to time, but they refused to do anything more drastic to remediate her behavior. Failure to act fails to inspire. Unfortunately, I did not believe that leadership would take the actions necessary to resolve a toxic situation. Additionally, it looked like the direction of the business would be to innovate with the rise of web-based media, and so I moved on.

After being recruited into this hospitality chain on the promise of upward mobility for the sacrifice of working weekends, it became clear after several months that this was an empty promise. After a year or so, I left that company to venture out on my own. With the support of my brother and good friend, I launched my first business: Silverstone Innovations. This marketing consulting company sought to use online campaigns to boost sales for small businesses. Looking back, we were too early and working with the wrong kinds of companies for what we offered. When my partners and I went our separate ways, I joined the workforce at a sales consulting firm.

Perhaps my most valuable previous work experience was at this consulting firm, where, as the Business Manager, I worked with emerging companies with over $25M in annual revenue. Being that this was a small firm, I wore many hats. I was responsible for bringing in new business, delivering sales and leadership training, as well as overseeing the implementation of the sales hiring and training processes within various companies. This role proved to be one of immense learning, but for me, the lack of work-life balance kept it from being a long-term career.

It seems like empty promises, disposable employees, high turnover, and negative company cultures are more common than uncommon in my experience. I could tell you countless more stories of business owners or colleagues who lie, manipulate, and make empty promises they cannot deliver on. That said, as I reflect on my windy path to entrepreneurship, I realize that more than anything, this is what I wanted to change.

If you're reading this, I hope your organization doesn't relate to any of the experiences I described above. Perhaps you are already part of a team that is functional, but you think there is room for people to improve. I want to help leaders guide individuals to their potential and help organizations of all sizes implement an infrastructure that engages employees and makes them feel valued. In turn, you'll enjoy watching a loyal team that is in it to win it. Such a team will put in more effort to generate ideas and help accomplish corporate objectives.

I'm proud to have partnered with Sylvia Henderson as the COO of MindTeam Solutions. I'm applying my talent for business development, my desire to impact a positive corporate culture, and my passion for helping businesses and people grow. It's very fulfilling to help companies create engaged and high performing teams that support the organization's development and growth.

We believe that a positive, respectful, and collaborative company culture is essential to the growth and sustainability of any organization.

Now that you have read our stories, give some thought to how *yours* relates. Consider what motivates you to positively influence your people and your organization.

Additional suggested reading:

- You can read Sylvia's and Josh's expanded stories at MindTeamSolutions.com/internalmasterminds

Journal

What is *your* story of your experiences as an engaged, loyal, valued employee at various points in your career, profession, or jobs? Identify both positive and toxic experiences.

How do your experiences relate with either Sylvia or Josh? Both?

Within your organization, how are you creating an environment that promotes positive engagement?

Within your organization, where might you have toxic experiences that need to be addressed… immediately?

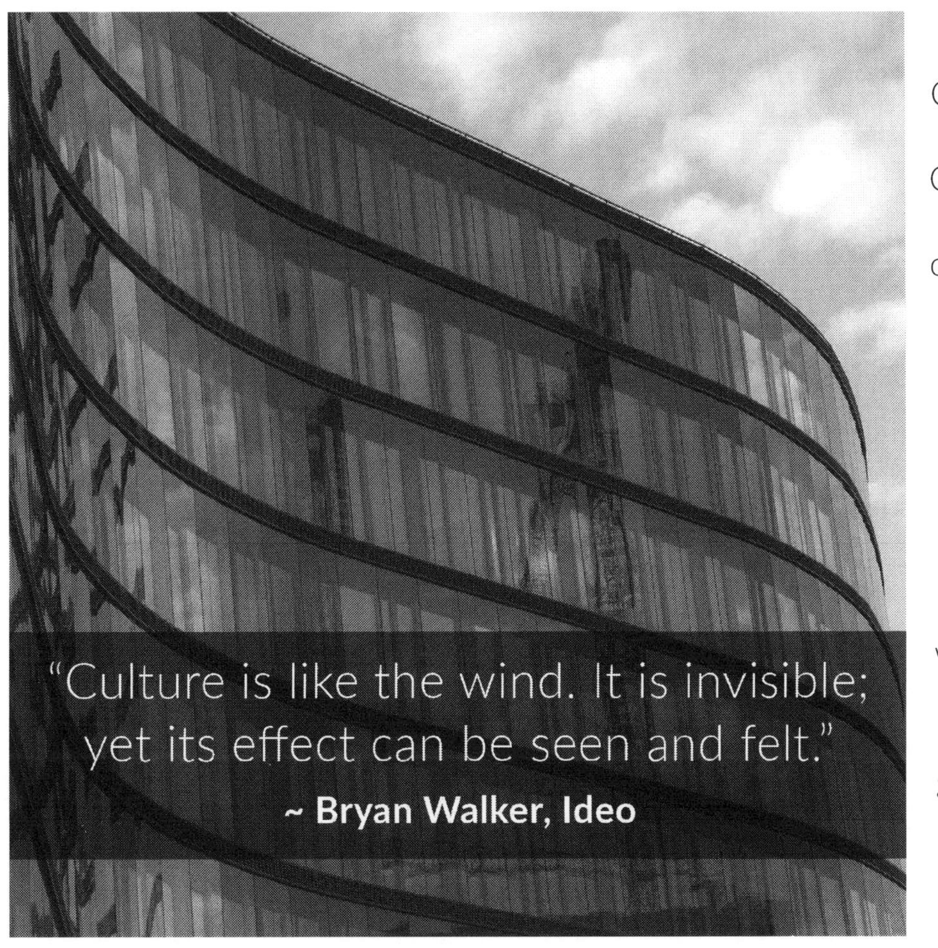

"Culture is like the wind. It is invisible;
yet its effect can be seen and felt."
~ Bryan Walker, Ideo

"Every CEO is in fact a Chief Cultural Officer. The terrifying thing is it's the CEO's actual behavior, not their speeches or the list of values they have put up on posters, that defines what the culture is."
~ Scott Berkun, Author, *Making Things Happen* and *The Dance of the Possible*

"Research indicates that workers have three prime needs: Interesting work, recognition for doing a good job, and being let in on things that are going on in the company."
~ Zig Ziglar

Chapter 4

Challenges Facing Organizations: Developing Talented Leaders

True business success comes when a company can deliver value to the customer while sustainably growing the organization. Meanwhile, the business must be able to meet the ever-evolving needs of their clients better than the competition can. Companies that achieve this success innovate quickly by tapping into their engaged, committed employees who work in a collaborative way with their colleagues to think critically in order to solve the next hurdle in front of them. Although many businesses know that employees thrive in a diverse, positive workplace, many well-intentioned business leaders do not know how to create and nourish this kind of culture. In some organizations there are systematic or unintentional silos cutting off communication between different departments, divisions, and teams.

The first step is top-level leadership that focuses on creating a strong foundation built on the organizations' vision and mission, translating into core values that permeate throughout the organization. In a good faith effort to improve efficiency, effectiveness, and profitability, executive leaders turn to one-off trainings, annual staff retreats, and motivational posters. Just

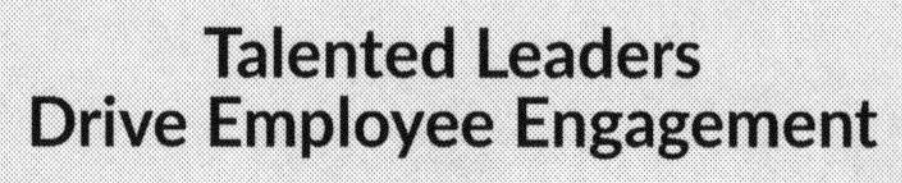
Talented Leaders
Drive Employee Engagement

Talented leaders and positive workplace environment

↓

Engaged employees

↓

Employees committed, dedicated, motivated to make organization a success

↓

Customer engagement

↓

Increased sales and profits

↓

Increased stock price / happy stakeholders

Based on Concepts from Dale Carnegie Training[2]

as the needs of clients evolve, so do the category of trainings companies need to consider in this market. While these types of trainings have been around for decades, the priorities of consumers and employees alike are not the same as they were decades ago.

Once leaders accept that the numbers of millennials (and the emerging generation) in the workforce dictate a shift in business priorities, they are already moving a step forward in the right direction. To achieve organizational visions and goals, companies must invest in and develop their teams. Despite organizational leaders throwing money at the "training solution," only 10% of employees report using what they learned at training sessions. Simultaneously, over 70% of employees self-report as disengaged.[1] Despite a multi-billion-dollar global training industry, these results have seen little to no long-term improvement. This is because the workforce is shifting to one whose defining characteristics include the need to feel valued, to contribute to the greater good, and to have a work-life balance while retaining advancement opportunities.

It's no small order, but whether your business goal is to sell your company where the buyers often consider the culture they are acquiring or you intend to do good in the world by giving people a wonderful place to spend the majority of their waking hours, shifting focus to training centered on emotional intelligence (EI) is a must. Although good leaders can be recruited, they must also be given the opportunity to continue their development. Additionally, you're going to need to develop leaders from within. The most effective leaders are alike in one definitive way: they all have a high degree of what has come to be known as emotional intelligence. According to the Carnegie Institute of Technology, research shows that 85% of financial success is due to skills found in EI while only 15% is due to technical ability.[3]

Although this concept may sound new to many readers, it's been around for quite a while. However, the changing make-up of the workforce is shifting its importance in the training landscape. In 1995, Daniel Goleman wrote a book called *Emotional Intelligence: Why It Can Matter More Than IQ*. EI is the capability of an individual to recognize their emotions and discern the feelings of others. Recent research and studies show that EI competencies are essential to leadership when this information is used to adjust thinking and guide behavior. Imagine how improved your customer interactions would be if your employees and team leaders honed these skills. Better customer interactions lead not only to increased revenue, but also to more satisfied employees more likely to work successfully with their colleagues towards common goals. There are five key components that make up EI; we introduce them below and discuss them in more detail in chapter 12, "Mindset Matters for Leaders and All of Your Employees."

Five Components of Emotional Intelligence

1. Self-awareness
2. Self-regulation
3. Motivation
4. Empathy
5. Social skills

The first component is self-awareness, which is your ability to recognize and understand your moods, emotions and drives as well as their effect on others. The second is self-regulation, the ability to control your impulses and moods, suspend judgments, and think *before* acting. Next is motivation, a passion to work for reasons beyond money or status, and to pursue these goals with energy and persistence. Then there is empathy, understanding the emotional makeup of other people you interact with. Last, these other components build the foundation of your social skills, your proficiency in managing relationships and building networks.[4]

Strong emotional intelligence can assist most people in both their professional and personal lives. For managers and leaders, they are critical to success. While some leaders are inherently "naturals," others may have all the abilities on paper yet struggle to produce results. Great executive leaders recognize these managers and invest in them. Investment in the right type of training leads to retention of talent, stability of leadership infrastructure, and ultimately confidence and growth in your front-line employees.

Our combined years of leadership training and experience have shown us that traditional training models of videos, worksheets, and one-off training retreats are not the most effective delivery methods for leadership development. Although these ideas introduce skills and concepts, leaders show the most improvement and growth with experiential learning. Simply stated, our experience shows that you need to witness good leadership and communication and then have the opportunity to *practice* it. Over time, this practice grows your emotional intelligence. Based in EI, strong communication and confident leaders enable organizations to live out their vision through their mission.

---

1. https://news.gallup.com/home.aspx
2. Dale Carnegie Training Center Paper: "What Drives Employee Engagement and Why It Matters". DaleCarnegie.com/assets/1/7/driveengagement_101612_wp.pdf
3. https://www.fastcompany.com/3047455/why-emotionally-intelligent-people-are-more-successful
4. "Emotional Intelligence in Leadership: Learning How to Be More Aware". www.MindTools.com. Article based on the book *Emotional Intelligence: Why It Can Matter More Than I.Q.* by Daniel Goleman.

Journal

What are the 3 biggest challenges you have with your employees?

Which of your current employees may become good leaders with proper training *and* practice?

Which departments or divisions may benefit from closer collaboration?

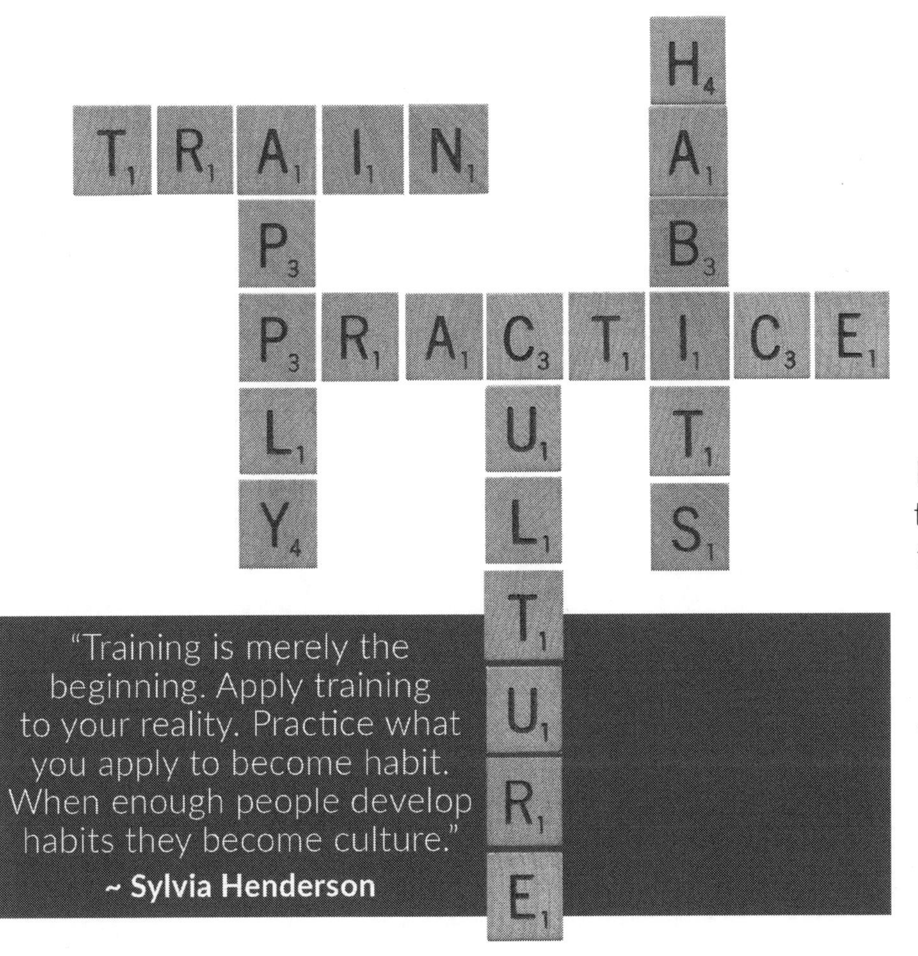

TRAIN
APPLY
HABITS
PRACTICE
CULTURE
"Training is merely the beginning. Apply training to your reality. Practice what you apply to become habit. When enough people develop habits they become culture."
~ Sylvia Henderson

"Tell me and I forget, teach me and I may remember, involve me and I learn."

~ Benjamin Franklin

"If you want to teach people a new way of thinking, don't bother trying to teach them. Instead, give them a tool, the use of which will lead to new ways of thinking."

~ R. Buckminster Fuller

"People grow best where they continuously experience an ingenious blend of challenge and support."

~ Robert Kegan

Chapter 5
Single Solutions Are a Mixed Bag

Why Training – and Other Short-Term Solutions – Are Not Enough

Conduct an internet search for the term "training not enough". My most recent search yielded over half a million results. That's a lot of searching for solutions beyond "just training".

As of this writing, the business environment involves five generations of employees and employers, exponential technological growth requiring rapid organizational and personal adaptability to change, diminishing interpersonal competencies, and an increasing demand to meet desired outcomes and stakeholder profitability. Employers look for holistic solutions. We use "holistic" for its meaning of relating to or concerned with wholes, or with complete systems rather than its parts, instead of its medical or spiritual meanings.

Large organizations seek ways to achieve the agility to pivot to match rapid market changes that small organizations can make with less bureaucracy.

Skills Top Executives and Hiring Managers Seek

Technical skills are important, yet as job requirements change with exponential technological developments, tech skills face obsolescence, automation, and specialized internal training in niche areas.

Skills most needed in a continually-shifting job market are "soft skills", or what we prefer to call interpersonal and thinking competencies – communication, team work, problem-solving. The ability to learn to learn and navigate the ambiguity of a career will prove most valuable to educational system graduates and employees in the long run.[1]

Organizational leaders typically seek and implement talent development solutions that include assessments, training, coaching, consultants, motivational posters, bonuses, and recognition events to improve their people's skills, engage and retain employees, communicate company culture, and provide inspiration. Each of these solutions has its place for meeting specific needs within an organization. None are enough in and of themselves to cause attitudinal and behavioral changes that enable an organization to thrive over time. They must be used in combinations together to achieve the desired outcomes.

Almost one-third (31%) of employees receive little formal training. 43% who receive training find it to be ineffective.[2] Training, like the other solutions mentioned above, is a one-and-done effort. Yes, these solutions may be repeated, combined, and scaled throughout the organization. Yet without long-term integration, practice, continual reinforcement, performance accountability and a culture of acceptance, trust, and adaptability to change, these solo solutions prove ineffective for long-term loyalty, idea implementation, culture permeation, and bottom-line impact.

Additional support beyond single solutions is necessary to transform knowledge, skills, and attitudes (KSAs) into sustained behaviors, performance, culture, and economic impact.

Clayton Christensen, author of *The Innovator's Dilemma* and *The Innovator's Solution*, notes that companies have to transform their management practices to be agile and lean in to how innovative people within their organizations want to operate. This also applies to transforming their approach to talent development solutions.

Tendayi Viki, author of *The Corporate Startup*, explains that the Lean Startup movement took root within the technology ecosystem.[3] Operational processes were developed and implemented to help innovators fail fast and pivot their businesses quickly as the economy, technology, and customer buying habits rapidly changed. Leaders in large organizations look to bring lean processes into their organizations after seeing the rapid growth of startups.

When front-line project teams in bureaucratic organizations seek to initiate innovative ideas, they typically find they are in organizations poorly structured to support new skills and innovative ways of working. Organizations that practice industrial-era, top-down hierarchical business models have long budget cycles, thick business binders, and incentives based on shareholder financial results. When innovative employees seek to take initiative and risk sharing new ideas, they are stifled by bureaucracy.

Entrepreneurship and innovation operate at different paces from that of large organizations. They follow a build-measure-learn loop process to make assumptions and take action, then use analytics to make evidence-based decisions. Sandra Yancey, CEO of eWomenNetwork, calls this a plan-do-review process that is key to her organization's multi-million dollar growth and success. This process enables teams to identify challenges and client needs, build appropriate solutions, and implement strategies efficiently to deliver value and meet leaders' desired outcomes.

A holistic solution integrates talent development approaches mentioned earlier in this chapter as well as a means of allowing employees to practice their skills, increase competencies, communicate across departments, live organizational credos and core values, develop leadership skills, take initiative, think critically, make informed decisions, and implement ideas. Employees feel more engaged in the organization's mission, stay longer, and treat their roles and responsibilities like entrepreneur owners of their slices of the business. Willis Towers Watson looked at 50 global companies and found that those with low engagement scores have an average operating margin of just under 10 percent, whereas those with the highest "sustainable engagement" scores have an average one-year operating margin of 27 percent.[4]

One example that confirmed the need for such a holistic solution came to us in a conversation with a talent development leader just prior to publishing this book. To honor confidentiality requests, we will change names. Her organization is a major government contractor with hundreds of people located across the USA. Margaret, the Talent Development Director, is responsible for training and development initiatives for both individual departments and the company as a whole. She notes that single training and coaching solutions work for meeting specific, targeted competencies and business issues. Yet she values a comprehensive strategy that includes cross-departmental, long-term, multiple-modality solutions. This complements the one-and-done talent development programs so that learned skills become habits, which become corporate culture, which transform business results.

What can such a holistic solution look like? Continue reading. You will extend your vision for such a solution in the next chapter.

---

[4] *Why Good People Can't Get Jobs: The Skills Gap and What Companies Can Do About It*. Peter Cappelli. Wharton Digital Press. ASIN: B079C8JZ19.

[1] "State of Workplace Training Study". Axonify. HRDive.com

[2] "Why Lean Startup Training Is Not Enough". Tendayi Viki. Forbes.com. #LikeABoss

[3] "How Employee Engagement Hits the Bottom Line". Harvard Business Review.

Journal

What do you do now to encourage and support employee engagement?

How long, on average, does your staff remain with your organization?

If you had to pivot your organization next week, how would you engage your staff to help make a transformation happen?

What is the cost to you and your organization – financial, legacy knowledge loss, and cultural – for failing to engage and retain your staff?

"Every time you state what you want or believe, you're the first to hear it. It's a message to both you and others about what you think is possible. Don't put a ceiling on yourself."
~ Oprah Winfrey

"You can't make radical changes in the pattern of your life until you see yourself exactly as you are now. As soon as you do that changes will flow naturally."
~ Henepola Gunaratana

"Have a vision. Be demanding."
~ General Colin Powell

Chapter 6

A Vision for Transformation – The Future of Your Workplace is Here Today

Research the phrase "future of work" and you will find in-depth reports, white papers, research, statistics, and executive overviews from reputable sources such as McKinsey & Company, Deloitte, The Brookings Institution, Forbes, The Economist, and many more.

Five "Future Now" Issues Your Front-Line Can Help Pivot When They Are Engaged

1. Internet of Things
2. Cyber Security
3. Artificial Intelligence (and Resulting Job Restructuring)
4. Outsourcing
5. The Cloud

In the Journal of Business and Management, a paper by Dr. Chandrakanta Sahoo and B. Venkata Prasad entitled "Talent Management: Issues and Strategies" notes that the dynamic, fast-changing nature of our world and workplace is best described by the acronym VUCA, which stands for Volatility, Uncertainty,

Complexity and Ambiguity. This VUCA world pushes Human Resources and Talent Development in a direction in which a power shift from the top-down hierarchy of employers, to employees on the front lines as knowledge workers, is in play.

Common themes and observations among these sources and from organizational development and leadership experts is that companies must undergo organizational transformation in the coming years to remain viable. Breaking news: the coming years are already here!

The following excerpt is from Joyce Gioia, a Strategic Business Futurist and the author of "The Herman Trend Alert".

> The Washington Post tells us that 71 percent of today's workers (in the United States) are looking for new jobs. On top of that, thousands of baby boomers are retiring every day.
>
> To stay competitive, companies need to make significant organizational changes to address skill shifts. What's needed is an emphasis on "continuous learning" for all workers and a transition to more "cross-functional and team-based work". Moreover, companies need to become more agile, in part by encouraging independent work.

Other shifts needed by HR and leadership

Leadership and human resources also must adapt to the changing workplace. Almost 20 percent of the companies surveyed said their executive teams lacked "sufficient knowledge to lead adoption of automation and artificial intelligence". Over 30 percent expressed concern about lacking the skills they needed for automation adoption which would hurt their future financial performance. They are right to worry!

Tightening labor markets for high-skilled workers

While low-skilled workers will continue to lose their jobs to automation, competition for high-skill workers will increase. This trend aggravates income inequality and reduces the number of middle-wage jobs. The McKinsey study reports that high-skilled workers are the most likely group to be hired and retrained—and see their wages rise.

Slower adopters will struggle to attract talent

Slower adopters will have more limited options. Nearly half of the companies surveyed believe all of the groups involved, including employers, communities, and workers, will need to cooperate to manage the large-scale retraining required to transition in the years ahead. Long overdue is the collaboration between firms and educators to reshape school and college curricula.

There are also roles for industry associations and labor unions to help build talent pipelines and promote cross-sector mobility. Governments must consider providing safety nets for transitioning workers by encouraging a shift to portable benefits rather than penalizing mobility. This portability of benefits can be meaningful for helping employers best utilize the talents and skills of workers across sectors.

Organizations of the Future
Firms that are agile will be rewarded with profitability; those remaining stagnant may not make it to 2030.[1]

For examples of companies that did not pivot to their market or to innovative solutions quickly enough, consider once-venerable names no longer in retail store or stand-alone businesses such as h.h.gregg, Blockbuster Video, Lionel Corporation, Compaq Computers, E.F.Hutton, Woolworth's, MCI WorldCom, and Toys-R-Us. Note: Some of these names have been acquired by other companies and still have online presences.

Now it is your turn to create or fine-tune your organizational vision for the transformation you imagine – or are in the process of making happen – so that your people feel they are valued contributors to your organization's progress and your organization's leaders realize their value to the bottom line over the next twenty years.

Vision Worksheet

You want or value the following attributes in your company.
Check-mark all that you visualize in the first column ("Visualized").
Then check-mark what you have in place in the second column ("In Place").

Visualized	In Place	Agile Attributes
		Complete organizational assessment so that everyone speaks the same language and understands how to relate to one another
		Engaged employees who feel that their contributions are valued and make a difference to the organization's outcomes
		Loyal employees who stay with your company two years or longer
		Opportunities to practice competencies learned and enhanced in training programs so that they become habits

		Opportunities to apply lessons learned, long-term
		Establish trust; work together; collaborate
		Solve problems using critical thinking
		Have, and take advantage of, opportunities to grow and use strengths
		Communicate across departments to eliminate departmental silos
		Communicate effectively horizontally (across) and vertically (up and down), both within and outside the organization
		Freedom to introduce and implement ideas
		Multiple generations work well together
		Access to experts to address specific leadership, management, and executive issues
		Create leadership opportunities for front-line and middle-management staff
		Anything else to add to your vision?

The gap between what you have in place now and your vision is what you might consider filling with a long-term, holistic solution in order to ensure your organization is agile enough to respond to the changing environment of the future of work, today.

The full McKinsey & Company report is worth reading and taking to heart as we provide you with a solution to identified gaps that can derail your organization's survival.

Additional suggested readings:

- "State of Workplace Training Study". Axonify – 2017. HRDive.com
- "Unleashing the power of small, independent teams". McKinsey Quarterly.
- https://www.mckinsey.com/business-functions/organization/our-insights/unleashing-the-power-of-small-independent-teams

---

[1] With permission from Joyce Gioia. Source: "The Herman Trend Alert," by Joyce Gioia, Strategic Business Futurist. 336-210-3548 or www.hermangroup.com. The Herman Trend Alert is a trademark of The Herman Group, Inc." The Herman Group, 7112 Viridian Lane, Austin, Texas 78739 USA

Journal

Where are the gaps between your vision and where your organization is now for meeting your "people needs" for the future of your workplace?

What is your full vision of where your organization will be in twenty years?

To what area determining the future of your workplace can you give singular focus for radical transformation in your organization?

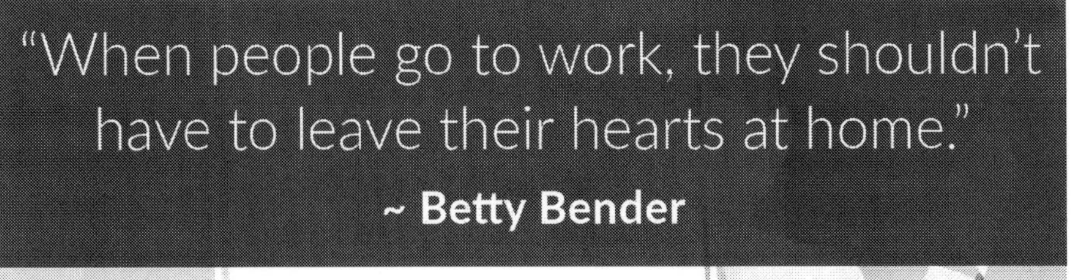

"When people go to work, they shouldn't have to leave their hearts at home."
~ Betty Bender

"I came to see, in my time at IBM, that culture isn't just one aspect of the game, it *is* the game. In the end, an organization is nothing more than the collective capacity of its people to create value."

~ Louis Gerstner, Past IBM CEO

"It starts at the top. Leaders set the pace and cadence of an organization. They are always being watched. Learn how the leadership lives their lives. Typically, the core values of an individual in their personal lives are reflected in their company and leadership."

~ Marissa Levin, CEO, Successful Culture

Chapter 7
It's About Culture

Much ink and digital ones-and-zeros are written about corporate and organizational culture. In our studies and consulting practices we've unearthed differing definitions and thoughts on what constitutes culture in an organization, how to create "it", and what effect having a defined or implied culture has on bottom-line results.

We lack the bandwidth in this book to dig deeply into a study of organizational culture. There is, however, some consistency in perspectives of what constitutes an organization's culture, how culture influences employee behaviors and attitudes, and the financial implications of culture being well-understood and lived by everyone in the organization.

The consistent point in defining the culture of an organization embraces the idea that organizational – or corporate – culture encompasses the environment and both physical and social norms, that influence behaviors, mindsets, visual presentation, interactions, and "feel" of and for the people who are part of the organization. Culture defines "how to be" in an environment. Factors that define an organization's culture include the founders' vision, core values, norms, systems, symbols, language, assumptions, beliefs, and habits.

Culture as North Star

The North Star, or Polaris, which appears as a fixed point in the sky, is a primary navigation point for multiple modes of travel. It appears as a celestial constant – a focal point upon which travelers can depend to guide them.

So too can culture, defined by vision, mission, and core values, serve as the guide and constant for navigating the organizational universe.

One of our strategic partners, SOAR Community Network, calls this corporate DNA, as culture is the essence of an organization's existence and longevity. Others call culture their North Star or Polaris Principles. In astronomy the North Star is a guiding star that is used as a reference point in navigation.

Differing perspectives on corporate culture resemble the chicken-or-the-egg conundrum…whether culture is set intentionally from the top of the organization and influenced down to the front lines or whether the people set the culture and it becomes an organic entity.

Organizational culture relates to the people within the organization because people typically want to work at places that set them up to succeed. They actively look to improve the organization. A culture where people can thrive includes elements such as high levels of engagement, people in positions that align with their strengths and natural talents, and opportunities to continually grow and learn.

A Gallup study notes that high engagement is correlated with nearly every important measure of organizational health, productivity, retention, safety, customer satisfaction and profits. A highly engaged organization can see 18% higher revenue per employee compared with the average. Yet fewer than 1% of organizations have all of these elements of a positive culture.

To create or deepen a culture of innovation and agility, direct engagement, strengths, messaging, systems, retention and growth efforts and investments must be directed toward processes, programs, and outcomes that promote creativity, ideation and risk-taking to achieve desired outcomes.

Another purpose of a well-defined organizational culture is to serve as a guide and leverage point for change when two or more organizations merge. When organizations merge or acquire one another, their two cultures must become one, and everyone in the new structure must understand how to "be" in their new universe. A platform where members of each organization, across hierarchical levels, can come together as one to work through issues and share ideas can serve as a catalyst for transformation so that the new entity thrives.

Sylvia experienced challenges of integrating two cultures when the agile tech company for which she worked acquired a conservative, bureaucratic company with a different culture. Their way of being in her company included cross-departmental communications, ideation at informal conversation pits throughout the building, open-space cubicles, casual attire, and beer parties on Fridays. The people in the company they acquired were accustomed to formal meetings with defined agendas, offices assigned by positions on the org chart, business suits, and pre-scheduled networking events.

When they initially judged each other's cultures as positive or negative, they were frustrated and angry with their peers, their customers felt it, and the new entity lost business and valuation. Once they, at the employee level, found ways to learn the other's histories and influencers, they collaborated and became their own internal brain trust that lead to a positive organizational transformation.

Our solution for creating an agile and engaged culture is through groups – not simply project teams which are the typical concept of implementing teams in the workplace, but intentional high-performance peer groups that transcend projects, involve employee performance, and invite welcoming ideas and taking risks. The solution encompasses the power of the third mind throughout the organization.

Additional suggested readings:

- https://soarcommunitynetwork.com/corporate-dna/
- *My Company ROCKS! Eight Secrets to a Growth-Driven Culture That Keeps Employees Happy & Engaged.* Author: Marissa Levin. ASIN #B007GTWK02

- https://www.forbes.com/sites/williamcraig/2014/10/24/what-is-company-culture-and-how-do-you-change-it/#15df7526b308
- https://www.investopedia.com/terms/c/corporate-culture.asp
- Harvard Business Review articles and papers at https://hbr.org
- *The Culture Cycle: How to Shape the Unseen Force that Transforms Performance.* James L. Heskett. Pearson FT Press. ISBN-13: 978-0134387079.

Journal

What does "organizational culture" mean for you?

How is culture cultivated in your organization?

Is it working? If yes, where and how? If no, where and how not?

If you could change, improve, or replace one thing that influences your organization's culture tomorrow, what would it be?

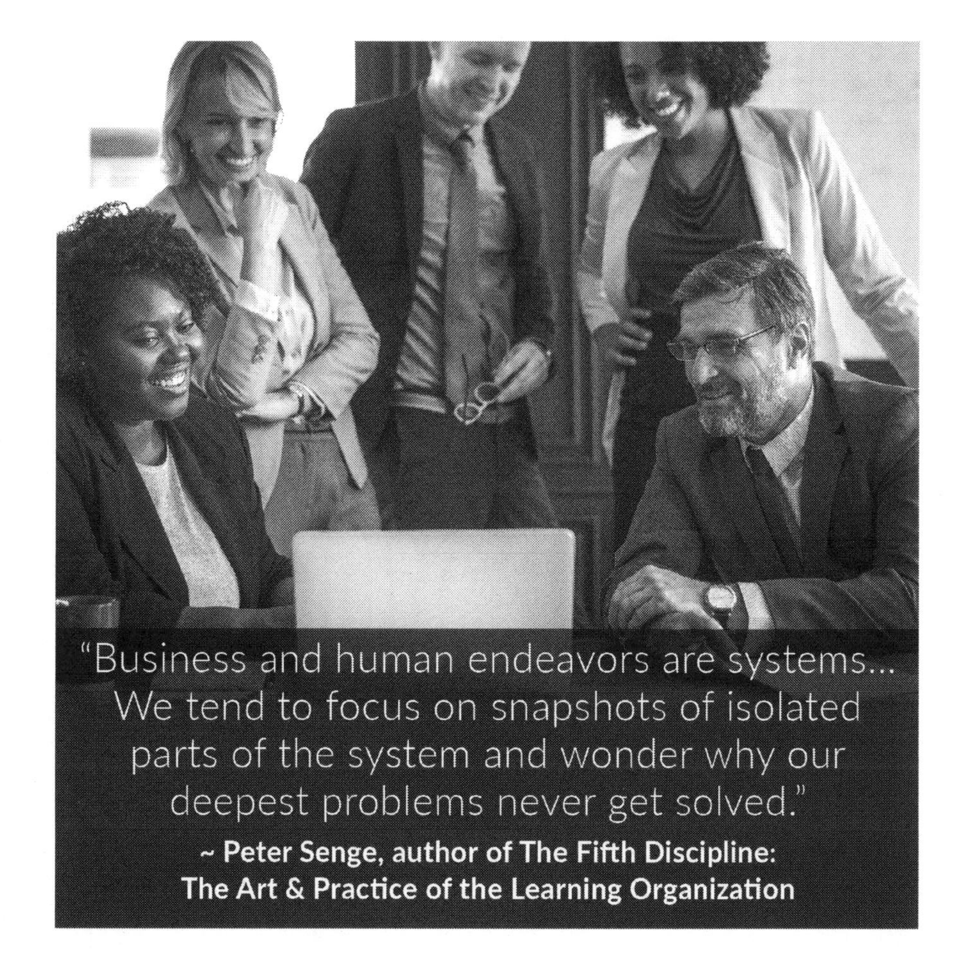

"Business and human endeavors are systems... We tend to focus on snapshots of isolated parts of the system and wonder why our deepest problems never get solved."
~ Peter Senge, author of The Fifth Discipline: The Art & Practice of the Learning Organization

"There are only three measurements that tell you nearly everything you need to know about your organization's overall performance: employee engagement, customer satisfaction, and cash flow. No company, small or large, can win over the long run without energized employees who believe in the mission and understand how to achieve it."

~ Jack Welch, Past CEO of General Electric Corp.

Chapter 8

Intentional, Collaborative Peer Groups

Findings from research and consulting firm Great Place to Work, which surveys 500,000 U.S. employees at nearly 800 public and privately owned companies annually[1], consistently reveal that companies where people say they feel their ideas are sought out and valued tend to yield greater revenue growth and employee productivity. Companies that score in the top quartile on key performance indicators generate, on average, more than five times the revenue growth of companies in the bottom quartile. Employees are asked how often they are included in strategic decisions, whether they feel management is interested in their ideas, and whether they are encouraged to try new approaches to their work.[2]

Confirming the power of intentional, collaborative peer groups to engage and retain employees and disseminate corporate culture through a hierarchical structure, one major grocery store chain with 48,000 employees nationwide has "innovation teams" consisting of front-line employees and headquarters leadership. These teams create new programs and ideas that are tested in local stores before they are launched company-wide. A drug company holds forums where staff members nominate new drugs and receive feedback as to the viability of pursuing new research and product development.

Sow Seeds that Grow

The "Parable of the Mustard Seed" has faith-based origins, yet holds a universal message. From a tiny mustard seed grows a tremendous tree.

Ideas and issues flow freely when intentional, collaborative groups provide a platform that encourages trust and openness. The analogy to the parable is that from small beginnings of many ideas and issues, great growth, innovation, and transformation can happen in organizations that host such groups and encourage a culture of collaborative intelligence.

The Vice President of Innovation & Development at Great Place to Work notes that companies must open their mindsets about what employees can offer in the way of new ideas and improvements. He goes on to say that leaders who do not honor this are going to miss out.

Each of the four words in this chapter's title is important to the success of the specific group platform we introduce to you.

"Intentional" relays the purposeful nature and qualities of the group to both the individuals who participate in the group as well as the organization hosting them. Successful groups are formed with the intention of being productive for both participants and organization. Groups have processes and systems that guide how they operate.

"Collaborative" dictates how people communicate and behave. Group members work together while in sessions, sharing ideas, expressing concerns and issues, helping each other resolve challenges, gaining clarity to turn ideas to reality, and valuing their strengths. Members share resources that help other members.

Learning takes place while the group works on a member's specific issue as well as when other members listen and participate in the interaction. New opportunities may become known and members may discover ways in which working together across departments can minimize costs, time, and resources to create efficiencies for the organization.

"Peer" infers that during group sessions, everyone in the group considers one another peers and colleagues rather than staff, administrative personnel, managers, executives, or

Characteristics of successful groups include:

- Differing perspectives that allow participants to see issues each otherwise would not see alone. There may not always be agreement, yet perspectives are conveyed with respect.
- Mutual support. Group members within an organization understand what really goes on behind the scenes and provide support to one another.
- Accountability through commitments and follow-up. When group members know they will meet regularly with each other, they tend to honor each other's time and hold each other to their respective commitments.
- Strong leadership. Group members represent a spectrum of personalities, ways of working, communication styles, goals and motivations. Cohesiveness can result when strong, trained leaders facilitate group interactions.
- Speak the "same language". Assessment results allow use of relational language and understanding of each other's strengths.

other hierarchical positions in the organization. Peer also implies that members are aligned in mindset and intention of service and participation. Members check egos at the door and what is discussed in group sessions remains within group sessions. Confidentiality is of utmost importance for instilling the trust among group members that is imperative for success.

"Group" means multiple people are involved. Individuals are not working alone when they are members of the group. They participate, make commitments to the group, and practice positive group behaviors. They meet live, whether in-person on location or virtually due to their multiple physical locations.

Groups and the individual group members become stronger when they are supported in other ways. The most important support is from the executive leadership and founders / owners of the organization. Leadership must create an environment that welcomes, supports, and communicates results from group input. Other supports include specialized training, developing group facilitators to be strong leaders, and having access to development resources and expert consultations when needed.

A key competency that companies need now and for the future is people who are good at complex problem solving. Radical transformation usually lacks a clear, predetermined roadmap. People have to get out of their own heads and get feedback from each other to develop ideas and strategies and to solve problems.

Another important competency is coordinating with others and managing people. The ability to work with people of diverse backgrounds and experiences is critical to an organization's success. Well-managed group platforms provide such opportunity in an open, trusting environment. Creativity, critical thinking, and decision making are other important competencies that employees and leaders develop and practice through group participation.

When you create the platform, processes, and resources that enable such groups to operate regularly and consistently over time, you create a culture of engagement, collaboration, valued contributions, and loyalty that leads to profitability and sustainability.

---

1. Great Place to Work. https://www.greatplacetowork.com/best-workplaces

2. "Why Innovation Is a Team Sport". Wall Street Journal. https://www.wsj.com/articles/why-innovation-is-a-team-sport-1533732288

Journal

What peer group experiences have you had professionally?

Identify some of the positive aspects of your peer group experiences. What made them work specifically for you?

What, if any, aspects of peer groups left you frustrated and feeling like the groups were unproductive?

If you started the "perfect peer group", what would it look like?

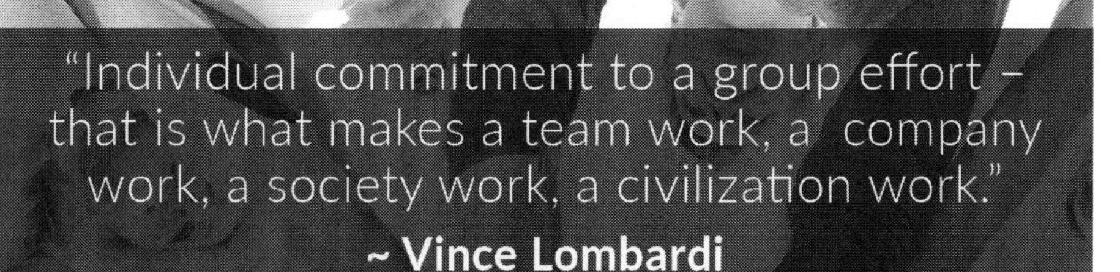

"Individual commitment to a group effort – that is what makes a team work, a company work, a society work, a civilization work."
~ Vince Lombardi

"The strength of the team is each individual member. The strength of each member is the team."
~ Phil Jackson

"Keep away from people who try to belittle your ambitions. Small people always do that, but the really great make you feel that you, too, can become great."
~ Mark Twain

"All business is personal. Make your friends before you need them."
~ Robert L. Johnson, BET Media Group

Chapter 9

Introducing the Idea MindTeam™ Platform

The practice of forming groups to solve issues, share ideas, and hold members accountable to their intentions is a popular approach implemented by coaches, consultants, and other transformational experts in the form of advisory and mastermind groups. Typically entrepreneurs, business owners, and executives form and participate in such groups, realizing individual business, career, and life benefits by doing so.

These groups vary widely in their formats and operations. We find, and have participated in, groups that range from week-long gatherings of hundreds of people led by celebrity personal development experts and their teams, to five entrepreneurs who meet quarterly at rotating locations around the world, to virtual video-conferenced sessions that are part of a consultant's program offering following a finite schedule. Few such groups strictly follow the tenets laid-out in Napoleon Hill's original edition of his book *Think and Grow Rich.*[1]

Project teams within organizations typically work together towards a specific desired outcome. They then either disband with members returning to their siloed departments or regroup to work towards the next desired outcome.

The structure and intent of Idea MindTeam™ groups harken back to Mr. Hill's original mastermind success philosophies so as to avoid confusion with other types of groups. The concept of Idea MindTeams originated when we authors, as entrepreneurs and founders of our respective businesses, studied success principles of personal development and business experts and formed a small mastermind group with other entrepreneurs. We needed to get out of our own heads and come together for ideation, collaboration, and support as peers because we normally worked alone. Our intention was to develop supportive relationships with each other and have them in place before we needed them. The sum of the relationships became our team of minds who helped us implement our business ideas. Thus we branded our group as our Idea MindTeam group.

Other entrepreneurs asked to form their own Idea MindTeam-branded groups as they saw the value of such groups in growing their businesses and themselves. They also liked that we had a documented system of processes, tools, and supports for productive sessions already developed and successfully implemented. They did not have to figure things out through trial and error, wasting time and money themselves.

Networking with and receiving messages from business leaders about employee engagement, retention, and corporate culture challenges caused us to realize that Idea MindTeam groups are unique solutions to such challenges in organizations as well.

The purpose of an Idea MindTeam group is to serve as a safe forum for its members to solve problems, get clarity on and work through issues with which they struggle, and put their ideas into the open to receive feedback and hear different points of view; in other words, the goal is to get out of their heads and have others help them in ways they would not accomplish working on their own. Employees can get suggestions and help from their peers who have varying experiences and strengths without fear that their bosses will think less of them if they are struggling with aspects of their jobs. Members engage in critical thinking processes, listen to their peers, ask questions that dig deeper into situations than initially presented, and freely share creative approaches to solutions.

Idea MindTeam group members come to trust each other and care about each other's progress and performance in their organization. Managers and bosses find they can release their tendencies to micromanage and spend more of their energies on the personnel and business development tasks appropriate to their levels. Group members return to their roles and responsibilities better able to tackle challenges, meet commitments, and work with others after getting help with the roadblocks that stymie them. They are referred to resources they might not otherwise know about.

Yes, implementing Idea MindTeam groups takes time and resources. However, as a solution to employee engagement, retention, siloed communications, and culture issues prevalent in organizations and the hits to bottom lines due to these issues, the value of such groups outweighs their investment.

Idea MindTeam platform differentiators include:

- Longevity – they are long-term implementations.
- Systems and processes – operations and resources are defined and documented.
- Replication – able to add groups within and throughout an organization, limited only by the number of people in the organization and the vision, perceived value, and desired outcomes of its leaders.
- Facilitation – specific training and resources are required for successful group facilitation that also serve as experiential leadership development opportunities beyond the group.
- Group size – a limit to the number of members in each Idea MindTeam group allows for all individuals to participate and become accountable.
- Comprehensive group supports; holistic talent development solutions – the Idea MindTeam group is the foundation of the platform, yet additional supports such as assessments and targeted training and consulting are part of the platform.
- Cross-departmental – each Idea MindTeam group consists of individuals from multiple

departments and, if appropriate, across multiple levels of the organization.

- Productive and action-oriented – agendas and logistics of the group disallow drama, gossip, personal agendas, organizational politics, and wasted time.
- Focused – designed to achieve individual progress and contribution towards organizational goals, bottom-line results, and founder / owner / leadership desired outcomes.

Value of Implementing Idea MindTeam™ Groups:

- Improve performance
- Increase productivity
- Minimize mistakes
- Refer resources, save time and reduce expenses
- Collaborate
- Cross-communicate between departments
- Be seen and recognized for strengths
- Practice leadership skills
- Apply competencies learned in training programs
- Take ownership of transformational processes from within
- Message and language practice and application

Distinguish Idea MindTeam groups from coaching, training, consulting, therapy sessions, networking groups, or performance evaluations. The Idea MindTeam group experience is laser-focused on issue processing, ideation, experiential talent and leadership development (practice), critical thinking and decision-making, and accountability to commitments. Such experiences, practiced consistently and repeatedly over time, engage participants in the group in ways that promote connection and interaction with diverse demographics of group members, open minds to different perspectives, engender trust and civility within the organization, and create a collaborative culture that enables the business to innovate, pivot when needed, and thrive.

---

[1] Napoleon Hill biography. https://en.wikipedia.org/wiki/Napoleon_Hill
Napoleon Hill Foundation: All things Napoleon Hill and his teachings. http://www.naphill.org/

Journal

Consider your network of people on whom you can call to bounce around ideas and to guide and help you throughout your professional journey. Identify at least one person by name for each category of your personal Idea MindTeam™ network. Where you have gaps, find and cultivate a relationship with such a person before you need her or him.

MindTeam	Who is your go-to person?
M entor (someone coaching and guiding you)	
I ntimate (friend or buddy)	
N etwork (outside your immediate silo, or even outside your organization)	
D iverse demographic (someone different from you)	
T eammate (peer or colleague)	
E xecutive (high-level position in your organization)	
A dministrator (assistant who helps you with administrative tasks)	
M entee (someone *you* coach and guide)	

An Idea MindTeam group provides your staff similar value and benefits of connection.

"The productivity of a work group depends on how the group members see their own goals in relation to the goals of the organization."
~ Ken Blanchard

"Coming together is a beginning, staying together is progress, and working together is success."
~ Henry Ford

"Cooperation is the thorough conviction that nobody can get there unless everybody gets there."
~ Virginia Burden

A small group of thoughtful people could change the world. Indeed, it's the only thing that ever has.
~ Margaret Mead

Chapter 10

How Idea MindTeam™ Groups Operate

The primary prerequisite for Idea MindTeam™ groups to be effective is the support and blessing of your organization's leadership and executive team. Implementing an Idea MindTeam platform is a top-down invitation that reinforces an open, risk-approving, idea-accepting, front-line-empowered work environment.

In order for the platform to work for employees and the organization, people must feel that issues and ideas they bring to the table, questions they ask, and uncertainty or fear they express in meetings will not be held against them or their performance evaluations. To the contrary, the results of participating in Idea MindTeam groups should enhance individual performances and serve as your internal brain trust to transform your organization. Group members must feel that their ideas, solutions, and intentions are supported or, at the very least, considered. If an action cannot move forward, communications channels must be in place so that the reasons are made clear.

Given that an Idea MindTeam platform is a "go" for your organization, here is how a typical group operates.[1]

An Idea MindTeam group meeting is a 2.5-to-3-hour event depending on the timeframe you, the group members, and the facilitator choose that works for your organization. The important aspect of timing is that meetings are scheduled consistently for the same day of the week and time of day, monthly or twice a month. One-month intervals between meetings are the longest recommended periods of time for the Idea MindTeam program to remain effective. This consistency and regularity allows group members to schedule their calendars for recurring meetings. They come to expect their Idea MindTeam group meetings at the specified timing and block their calendars from other commitments.

A trained facilitator coordinates meeting logistics, manages the meeting process, and performs follow-up activities. Ideally, facilitators are existing leaders, or people with leadership potential whom you want to further groom through leadership experience, within your organization. They must receive training on how to facilitate a work group rather than a classroom learning experience. While some facilitation skills are similar, getting members of a group to positively interact with each other over a long period of time and ensuring productive results requires skills different from facilitating a class.

If your groups have a virtual element because your organization is spread across multiple locations, the facilitator must also be able to operate the virtual tools. Such training can be done either from existing programs in your organization or from external sources.[2]

At the appointed meeting time, the facilitator starts the meeting on time. Managing time, group interaction, and members' mindsets are all key to Idea MindTeam group effectiveness.

The meeting starts with an agenda review and getting participants into a focused, positive, "all-in" mindset so that they fully participate and serve.

The group then moves into its primary purpose – issue processing and ideation. Up to four people have time – between 20-to-30 minutes each – to be in the spotlight per meeting. Due to the number of people in a group, everyone has a spotlight opportunity over a span of two-to-three meetings. Those who do not spotlight in a particular meeting still reap huge benefits from participating in the discussions and learning from others' situations.

The spotlight sessions encompass business or professional issues and ideas directly related to group members' jobs, roles in the organization, or direction the organization is heading as it relates to their responsibilities and contributions. No gossip; no personal dramas; no political maneuvering. The facilitator manages the timing, issue processing, and ideation procedures for each interaction.

Meetings may also include a short education session that addresses knowledge, skills, mindset, or aspects of organizational culture that members can apply to their job performance after the meeting.

What can derail a group setting?

- Politics
- Hierarchical positions in the company creating distrust; fear
- Relationship disfunction
- Feelings disrespected; judgements
- Leadership inexperience
- Negative experiences past and present
- Dominant personalities
- Diverse backgrounds poorly integrated
- Positioning for power
- Lack of respect for each other
- Lack of appropriate & applicable facilitation skills
- Poor discipline within group
- Non-committal participation; everyone not "on board"
- Stress, pressure, and deadlines
- Individual insecurities
- Negative mindsets
- Ineffective group leadership

Near the end of a meeting, each spotlighter chooses to commit to at least one action resulting from their spotlight session. She or he then selects an accountability partner in the group with whom they will follow up between meetings to hold to their commitments and get additional help if needed. Meetings wrap up with group operational items to discuss and a motivational or inspirational message with which to conclude.

The Idea MindTeam group process, repeated consistently over time, begets staff who become stakeholders in your organization's success and leaders who contribute positively to your organization's future outcomes.

---

[1] Watch an example of an Idea MindTeam™ group in action. This is an actual working group processing a member spotlight issue. It was recorded with the permission of the group's members. MindTeamSolutions.com/internalmasterminds

[2] MindTeam Solutions, Inc. has a full training and support package for certifying Idea MindTeam™ Facilitators. We can also provide facilitators trained specifically to the Idea MindTeam process.

Journal

What processes or programs do you have in place that engage and challenge employees at their performance levels?

How can they be scaled to your entire organization?

Where in your organization do you see implementing an Idea MindTeam™ platform solution yielding the greatest effect on engagement, retention, and culture? In what ways?

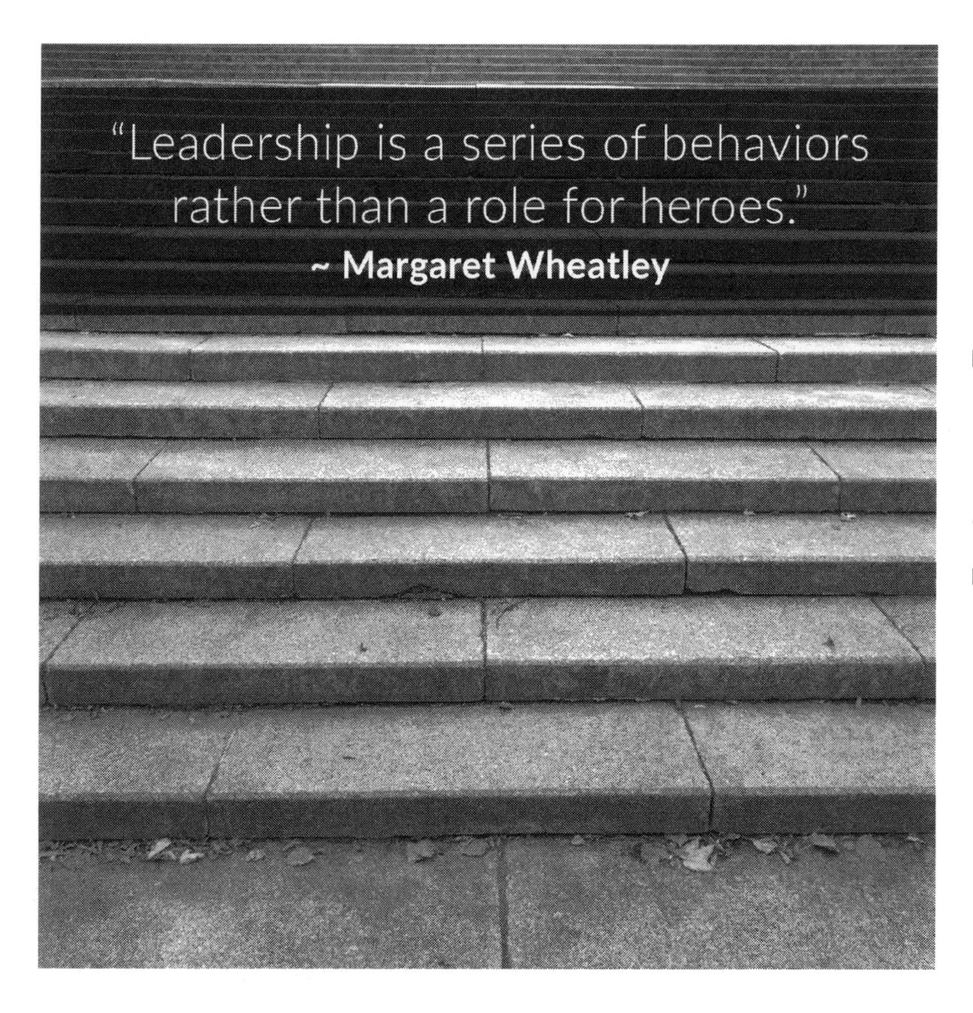

"Leadership is a series of behaviors rather than a role for heroes."
~ Margaret Wheatley

"A good leader takes people where they want to go. A great leader takes people where they don't necessarily want to go, but ought to be."

~ Rosalynn Carter

"There go my people. I must follow them, for I am their leader."

~ Mahatma Gandhi

"Serving others prepares you to lead others."

~ Jim George

Chapter 11

Leadership Development – The Facilitator Opportunity

In previous chapters we explained what Idea MindTeam™ group facilitators do and suggested whom you might select within your organization to serve as such. Be open to people volunteering to be facilitators as they realize the benefits that such opportunities afford to their career development and success goals.

Let's look at the characteristics, qualities, and competencies of an effective leader and how such a leader can fulfill a servant leadership role as an Idea MindTeam group facilitator. Serving as a facilitator is an excellent vehicle for leadership development and strengthening.

Servant leadership is an ancient leadership philosophy. Traditional leadership generally involves a hierarchy where the exercise of power is by people at the "top of a pyramid" in an organization. By comparison, the servant-leader puts the needs of others first and helps people develop and perform at their highest levels possible. Passages relating to such a leadership philosophy date back to the Tao Te Ching, attributed to Lao-Tzu, who is believed to have lived in China between 570-90 BC.

The modern interpretation and adoption of this leadership philosophy stems from the phrase "servant leadership" coined by Robert K. Greenleaf in his essay "The Servant as Leader," published in 1970[1]. It was further popularized and promoted by management expert Peter Drucker, founder of the Drucker Leadership Institute[2]. The Drucker Institute is the organization that ranks Fortune 500, S&P 500, and other large-cap companies according to their overall effectiveness in areas such as employee engagement, retention, and corporate culture as they influence best places to work and their bottom line results, which are the areas that the Idea MindTeam platform addresses. [3] [4]

Idea MindTeam™ Facilitator is a Servant Leader. What characteristics are qualities of an effective Idea MindTeam facilitator? Someone…

- Who listens and empowers rather than dominates and tells group members what to do.
- With the ability to inspire ideas that collectively are more than the sum of individual parts (creating the "third mind").
- Who helps organizations and staff identify their higher purpose and encourages individual growth.
- Who embodies the competencies of:
  - listening
  - questioning
  - empathy
  - healing
  - awareness
  - persuasion
  - conceptualization
  - foresight
  - stewardship
  - commitment to the growth of people, and
  - building community.
- Seeking her or his own leadership growth and development while balancing a passion to serve their peers and their organization.
- Who steps up to challenges and takes on additional responsibilities that stretch their capabilities.
- Unafraid to make tough decisions and initiate difficult communications, with honor and respect for the affected people.
- Earning followers through her or his actions, attitude, and support.

These are also qualities of a servant-leader.

While the skills involved in successful group facilitation can be taught, they must be practiced and honed through leadership opportunities and experiences over time in order to become competencies. Facilitating Idea MindTeam groups provides a platform for doing so. Such talent development may be a prelude to promotions, increased visibility inside and outside the organization, and management and executive opportunities as existing leadership develops and implements succession planning for the future growth of the organization.

Additional suggested reading:

- See the full "Management Top 250 Report" and highlights at the Wall Street Journal website and https://www.drucker.institute/rankings/

---

1. *Servant Leadership*. Robert Greenleaf. Greenleaf Center for Servant Leadership. ISBN 0-8091-0554-3. http://www.greenleaf.org/
2. Peter Drucker. The Drucker Institute. https://www.drucker.institute/
3. The Drucker Institute rankings. https://www.drucker.institute/rankings/
4. The Wall Street Journal highlights from the Management Top 250 report. http://graphics.wsj.com/image-grid/management-top-250/

Journal

How is the concept of "servant leadership" manifested itself in your organization?

What can you – and do you – do to model servant leadership so that you set the tone for a leadership culture of *earning* followers?

What are the markers in your life - the people and events - that helped shape your thinking about servant leadership?

GREAT LEADERS BELIEVE THEY WORK FOR THEIR TEAM, AVERAGE LEADERS BELIEVE THEIR TEAM WORKS FOR THEM.

ALEXANDER DEN HEIJER

"Your attitude, not your aptitude, will determine your altitude."
~ Zig Ziglar

"If you correct your mind, the rest of your life will fall into place."
~ Lao Tzu

"Failure is the opportunity to begin again more intelligently."
~ Henry Ford

Chapter 12

Mindset Matters for Leaders and All of Your Employees

Leadership is a practical skill and a mindset that is developed. Leadership skills are learned from observing others as well as participating in social interactions with people of various power dynamics throughout your lifetime. Think about how you may communicate with a board member of your company relative to an intern. How does the conversation change?

Although your leadership style has naturally grown, it is possible to shift, change, and recreate new intentional habits. First, we need to bring awareness to some concepts we introduced earlier in this book falling under Emotional Intelligence (EQ). We'll begin with the concept of motivation and the reasons why we do what we do.

In Daniel Pink's book, *Drive: The Surprising Truth About What Motivates Us*, he submits that human motivation is largely intrinsic, that it is contained within. This opposes the old models of extrinsic factors driven by rewards and fear. Pink boils it down to three main ideas that truly motivate us:

Autonomy – To be self-directed and choose how we do things.

Mastery – To keep improving at something that's important to us.

Purpose – To do that which gives us meaning beyond ourselves.

Are you in a position where these motivators are true? Are you allowing the people who work underneath you to fulfill their own needs using these ideas as a guide? If the answer is yes to both, then so far so good! If the answer is no, then think about how you can change how things are currently done to adapt to what is needed.

When you are motivated, you are an engaged employee who is more likely to be producing at a high level. There is a commitment and willingness to do what it takes to get the job done. There is a desire to do a good job and help the company. And lastly, you initiate and take actions that help move things forward and be successful.

Every leader and employee also needs to have a level of self-awareness. This includes being able to gauge your emotional state and mood as well as knowing how they will affect others. Additionally, it's being able to accurately characterize and think about your own personal strengths and weaknesses. Lastly, it's the confidence you have in yourself to be who you need to be to accomplish your goals and achieve your desired outcomes.

Another leadership capability is self-regulation. Part of this is your self-control, your ability to manage your impulses and think before acting. It is also being conscientious and trustworthy so that you have integrity and other people know they can expect high quality effort from you. It also requires the quality of adaptability, being able to adjust to new conditions and circumstances.

As it pertains to being a successful leader, you not only have to have an understanding of yourself, but you also have to understand the emotional makeup of other people. This is called empathy. You have to understand where people are coming from, understand what matters to them, and take an active interest in their concerns.

This is also important to other employees within a company from an organizational awareness perspective. This is where you understand the company from top to bottom and inside out. This helps employees better understand their roles in the greater mission, vision, and objectives of the organization.

Lastly, your social skills and ability to manage relationships and build networks is an important leadership skill. This casts a wide net, but includes teamwork and being able to collaborate with others. On the other hand, it's also your ability to manage conflict with people in a professional and productive manner. It encapsulates communication, establishes bonds, and influences others to change.

If you've been a professional long enough, you may have been in a situation where an employee or a coworker has had a sudden unexpected death in their immediate family. How do you think they may have been feeling? This is empathy. How does the conversation of death emotionally effect you? This is self-awareness. How did you word what you said to this person? These are social skills.

What could hold you or someone else back from taking action is limiting beliefs. Along our personal and professional journeys, we've all had experiences that we've interpreted and remembered in a certain way. Although you've come this far, perhaps there are some beliefs that are untrue and limiting to your potential.

These limiting beliefs can be general feelings about the world, your situation, or the people around you. There may be certain things you accept as true without ever asking why. This is best illustrated by the pig roast story.

A little girl is watching her mom prepare a pig roast for the family. The mother cuts the butt end off of the pig and puts it on a separate tray. The girl asks, "Mommy, why do you cut the end off the pig and put it on a separate tray?" The mom says, "I don't know, that's how my mom used to make it, go ask her." The curious little girl goes to her Grandma and asks, "Grandma, when you make a pig roast, why do you cut the end off of the pig?" Grandma says, "well, that's just how my mom used to make it, ask Great Grandma."

The little girl is determined to get to the bottom of this, and goes to find her. "Great Grandma, when you make a pig roast, why did you cut the end off of the pig?" Great Grandma says, "well dear, in my old apartment the oven was very small. The pig roast was too large to fit on just one tray. I had no choice but to cut the end off the pig because otherwise it wouldn't fit in the oven."

This anecdote tells us a lot about human nature, habits, and behavior. It shows us that some of the things we do are simply because that's how it was done before. It may be how we originally learned it, but we need to be more adaptive. It starts with asking ourselves why we are doing what we're doing. This forces us to think logically about our actions, and it assures that we are doing things on purpose and for good reasons.

Some limiting beliefs that may be holding leaders back could be ideas like, "leaders always tell people what to do". A couple others may sound like, "never show emotion or vulnerability" or "leaders are born, not raised". Can you see how thoughts like these could prevent someone from learning, growing, and engaging with their team?

A good way to evaluate whether you have your own self-limiting beliefs is to spend some time reflecting on a situation or concept you believe to be true. Ask yourself where the idea came from. Also think about what if any evidence may contradict this belief. Consider whether you have any proof to believe this is true. Once you're ready to let go of it, take immediate action to do so in order to create positive momentum in a forward direction.

This leadership and growth mindset puts you, the individual, in control of your own process for effecting outcomes. It takes responsibility for yourself and others in order to yield a positive result for you and your team. It then comes to creating a platform to have those interactions and work together. This is why we have developed the Idea MindTeam™ program.

Journal

Is your leadership team practicing tenets of emotional intelligence?

Are your employees fulfilling their intrinsic motivation needs?

What assessments have you used to get a better understanding of yourself and others?

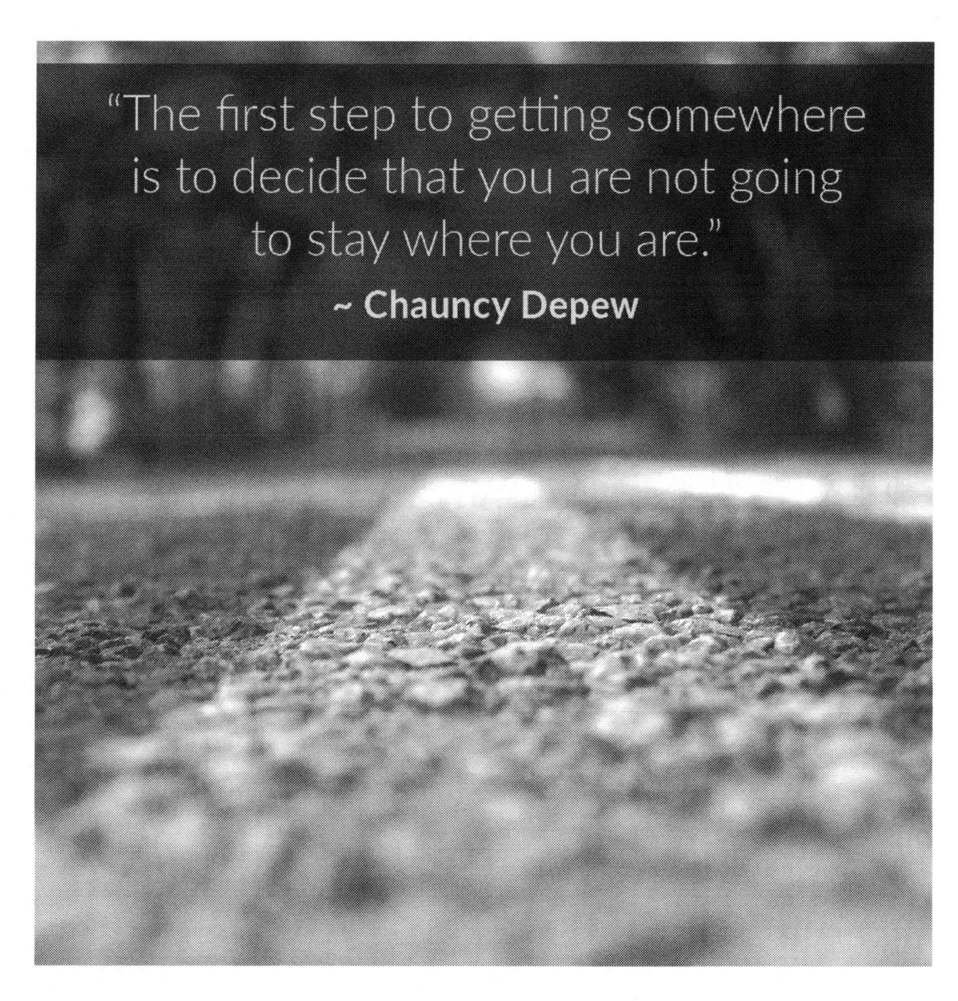

"The first step to getting somewhere is to decide that you are not going to stay where you are."
~ Chauncy Depew

"Just try new things. Step outside your comfort zone and soar."

~ Michelle Obama

"Successful people maintain a positive focus in life no matter what is going on around them. They stay focused on their past successes rather than their past failures, and on the next action steps they need to take to get them closer to the fulfillment of their goals rather than all the other distractions that life presents to them."

~ Jack Canfield

"An ounce of action is worth a ton of theory."

~ Ralph Waldo Emerson

Chapter 13

Where Do You Go From Here?

As we come to a close, let's review what you've covered and explored with us in this book, and discuss some actions you can take as a result moving forward. After all, what good is learning and discovery without action and implementation of the information? With a book physically pivoted, that is being formatted and printed in landscape rather than the "typical" portrait position, we wanted to show you that we believe in doing things differently and taking risks. Initiating meaningful change requires a shift in perspective and a consideration of new ways to approach things.

We started off this discussion by identifying the need for people and the value of employees connecting in organizations to enhance their job performance and the organizations' bottom-line results. Then we looked at Napoleon Hill's principle of the "third mind", and the power of getting people out of their own heads and into collaborative action. We, the founders and authors, also shared some of our experiences and explained why we're both passionate about sharing these ideas with you and playing a role in your organization's transformation.

We discussed some of the challenges within organizations and the concerns that leaders face as the workplace evolves. Unfortunately, bandages and one-and-done solutions, like an occasional training or posters on walls, are not enough to positively effect change that addresses these issues. Corporate culture needs to be a more holistic approach to complement and sustain engagement. The vision, mission, and values for a successful culture begin at the top, and it is the leaders' commitment to these ideals that dictates engagement, retention, and the overall health of your organization's culture and bottom line.

We believe that to make the necessary pivots to thrive in the future of the workplace, you have to engage your greatest asset: your people. We have found that collaborative peer groups with an intentional purpose and structure provide solutions to a number of organizational challenges including development of talent and leaders. Our Idea MindTeam™ platform provides a unique holistic solution for employee engagement, idea implementation, and organizational transformation. We shared how Idea MindTeam groups operate, as well as how you could start and implement a collaborative group.

This all sounds compelling, and you may be thinking, "Now what?" As mentioned above, you can design, create, and implement your own internal groups. However, we know you have enough on your plate, and we don't want you to have to sweat the details by implementing this on your own. That said, we unabashedly suggest that you contact us to explore how implementing the Idea MindTeam platform can benefit your organization. We begin with a simple conversation to establish a relationship before asking for your business.

We feel that the Idea MindTeam platform can benefit most organizations. Depending on your objectives, circumstances, and needs, our approach to launch and rollout will look different. For example, if your people have never taken an assessment, an assessment tool may help them get a better sense of themselves and their colleagues and be able to communicate using common terminology. Or perhaps your company is rebranding and you need to realign your vision, mission, and values before getting people working in the right direction; we would start there.

We believe that to keep and engage your talent, successful organizational leadership requires positive modeling of processes, actions, and behaviors. These ideas permeate from the top down and lead to a successful organization that thrives.

When groups come together, great things happen!

Next Steps

- Share *Internal Masterminds* with your colleagues and leadership team! We offer volume discounts from the retail price; order 50 books and receive a 50% discount. The order form is on page 151, and you can also contact us at info@mindteamsolutions.com.

- Contact us to have a conversation about your leadership development needs and organizational goals to see if implementing an Idea MindTeam™ platform within your organization can be a good fit.

- Bring us in to speak or host a workshop with your employees or leadership team.
  Topics may include:
  - The power of collaborative groups
  - The "third mind" and idea implementation
  - Leadership development
  - Pivoting organizational culture from the top, down
  - Emotional intelligence competencies for the future of the workplace, today
  - Idea MindTeam™ platform implementation

Appendix

Resource: Referenced Links

MindTeam Solutions, Inc. Website: http://www.MindTeamSolutions.com

MindTeam Solutions, Inc. Blog: http://MindTeamSolutions.com/blog/

Sylvia Henderson – Idea Implementation and Business Lessons Video Channel: https://SylviaHenderson.com/idea-pro-tips/

Josh Silverstone – Decision-Making and Critical Thinking Resources: http://AcesRaise.com/longtermstrategy

Book: *Delivering Happiness: A Path to Profits, Passion, and Purpose.* Tony Hsieh. Grand Central Publishing. Available at online and bricks-and-mortar bookstores. Physical book and Kindle. http://deliveringhappiness.com/book/

Book: *Think and Grow Rich – The Original 1937 Unedited Edition*. Napoleon Hill. Support the Napoleon Hill Foundation at this link. http://www.naphill.org/shop/books/think-and-grow-rich/

Book: *The 7 Habits of Highly Effective People*. Stephen Covey.
https://store.franklincovey.com/books-and-audio-360/the-7-habits-of-highly-effective-people-book

The Herman Trend Alert, by Joyce Gioia, Strategic Business Futurist. The Herman Group, Inc. Phone: 336- 210-3548. Web: http://www.hermangroup.com. The Herman Trend Alert is a trademark of The Herman Group of Companies, Inc. To subscribe, visit http://www.HermanTrendAlert.com.

Additional business and organizational development resources and readings

SOAR Community Network. Determine and communicate your corporate DNA and authenticate your brand messaging. https://soarcommunitynetwork.com/

Report: "Developing and Sustaining Employee Engagement". SHRM. Includes links and references to statistics from reliable sources, definitions and differentiations of terminology, and the case for creating a culture that fosters engagement and loyalty to increase the bottom line. https://www.shrm.org/resourcesandtools/tools-and-samples/toolkits/pages/sustainingemployeeengagement.aspx

Resource: Culture Example – MindTeam Solutions Inc.

Founders and leaders set culture and create the channels to spread it throughout the organization. The starting point for defining the culture of organizations is through leaders' visions and missions. Core values statements communicate the behaviors that lead to living the culture.

As an example, we openly and consistently communicate our vision, mission and values at MindTeam Solutions, Inc. to the public, our clients, and partners (see below). You will also see them online at http://MindTeamSolutions.com/about/.

Our Vision: At MindTeam Solutions, Inc. we value trust, celebrate diversity, and believe that every organization can create a corporate culture where individuals are respected and encouraged to contribute. We create safe environments inside organizations where all employees are empowered on a consistent basis to be intrapreneurial, have real conversations, openly share their ideas, use their unique skill sets, collaborate across functions, and move the best ideas forward for the benefit of the organization.

Our Mission: We facilitate organizational transformation and create strong corporate cultures through the foundation of our Idea MindTeam™ model platform. Our Idea MindTeam platform creates a high trust collaborative ecosystem for ideation, innovation, and problem-solving. This fosters employee engagement and professional growth while helping corporate leaders propel the company forward.

Our Core Values: At MindTeam Solutions, Inc. we value:

- Trust and honesty in relationships and interaction with each other.
- Respect for the individual at every level of the organization.
- Innovative ideas that when implemented make a positive impact on individuals, the organization, and society.
- Diversity of thought, status, culture, demographics, and strengths.
- Family, friends, and self-care as a balance to professional demands.
- Living a fulfilled life where every individual experiences what matters most to her/himself.
- Providing opportunities for personal and professional development, service to others, and achieving their goals.
- Open mindedness in creating environments where everyone is listened to, ideas are heard and considered without judgement.
- Honor system that is fair to everyone and does no harm.

These are also the core values we insist upon for every Idea MindTeam™ platform implementation. If a potential client, partner, vendor, or employee cannot accept and practice these (or similar), then we determine whether we are a good fit for each other. They are also on cards and other documentation so that all who do business with us know what we stand for.

Our commitment as co-founders – to each other, ourselves, and our clients – is to practice, live, and do business with those who share our core values. That is why they are "core".

Resource: Idea MindTeam™ Group Success Factors

Successful Idea MindTeam™ groups have:

- Structure; processes and procedures in place and documented
- Agreements and commitments; self-governing
- Core values aligned to the organization or Idea MindTeam™ program
- Trained Facilitators as leaders
- Mutual value and trust
- Ideas shared without judgement
- Honesty…with caring about others' successes
- Repeatability and replicate-ability
- Consistency; monthly or bi-monthly; day of week; specific start and stop times
- Small number of people in the group; attendance requirements → establish absentee limits
- Flexibility and adaptability

- Not just anyone is in the group
- Top-down organizational leadership support
- Participation → professional performance requirement
- Focused and productive → stay on-topic; spotlight professional / business issues and ideas
- Accountability and follow-up owned and expected of each group member
- Phones and distractions off
- Technology to allow for virtual participation → team spread around the country / world
- In the sessions, all are "equal" → no employee / manager / boss hierarchy
- Confidentiality strictly enforced → what happens in session stays in-session; with identified reporting process for fiscal responsibility and value confirmation to organization

About the Authors

Sylvia Henderson

Sylvia Henderson, CEO of MindTeam Solutions, Inc. and an idea implementation expert, moves clients' ideas out of their hearts and heads and into action for profit and purpose. She works with solo entrepreneurs and business founders and leaders who have a lot of ideas, heavy loads of responsibility, and teams who need to collaborate. She helps them to get focused, implement growth strategies, and be in intentional action to build businesses and leave legacies.

Sylvia brings over 40 years of experience and expertise – from IBM and AOL management, leadership, and corporate training; business consulting and ownership; non-profit Board leadership; and CEO advisory group chair service – to partner with clients on strategy and implementation as it involves their people. Through her consultation and leadership, she helps clients who believe their people are their greatest asset to identify and develop engagement and retention programs and increase their business development opportunities. Through her group facilitation she helps founders and business leaders collaborate, lead more effectively, avoid costly mistakes, and increase their bottom lines.

Sylvia is the author of multiple books including *Hey, That's MY Idea! How to Speak Up and Be Recognized for What You Know and Think*; speaks to audiences worldwide on how to make an impact and income with their ideas; hosts a cable television business program, internet radio and podcast, and Roku channel video programs; and facilitates long-term Idea MindTeam™ groups. She developed the worldwide Idea MindTeam program platform and implements the platform in organizations with her business partner and friend, Josh Silverstone.

Sylvia graduated with an MBA from the University of Pittsburgh's Graduate School of Business. She is a life member of the Girl Scouts of the USA and volunteers as an Adult Educator for her local Girl Scout Council. She is a member of a variety of professional associations including the National Speakers Association, Toastmasters International, and Leadership Montgomery (MD).

Away from business she enjoys riding her motorcycle and roller coasters, anything Star Trek™, and spending time with friends and family. She is the former mom of Welsh Corgis and lives with her life partner in the Washington, DC metro area.

Josh Silverstone

Josh Silverstone joins MindTeam Solutions as Chief Operating Officer with an extensive background in business development and helping organizations grow though more effective decision making. Prior to joining MindTeam Solutions, Josh founded Aces Raise and developed the Pokerpreneur® and NVRFOLD programs that use the strategies behind winning at poker to motivate leaders and teams and teach them better decision-making and risk taking skills.

Prior to providing training in this innovative way, Josh spent over a decade working in sales and marketing. Josh has a diverse business and industry background and has worked at every organizational level from front-line inside sales associate, to outside sales manager, to management consultant working with emerging companies generating more than $25M annually. Over that time, Josh served as a sales trainer, leadership developer, and manager of the sales hiring process.

This comprehensive experience has given him a unique perspective to bring to the Idea MindTeam™ platform, where integrating organizational levels in a collaborative, communicative environment is so crucial. Josh notes that working with Sylvia is a fulfilling and energizing experience. Together, they are excited to see their collective dreams manifest into a corporate vision where they have a significant impact on the growth and success of individuals and organizations.

At his core, Josh believes everyone has the ability to influence their life's outcome through focus, goal setting, and decision making. Josh loves to teach new tricks to his furry-son Griff, and help his newest human addition, Vivian, reach each of her developmental milestones. In his free time he enjoys golf, mountain biking, cooking, and rooting for DC sports teams. Josh lives in Silver Spring, Maryland with his loving wife Jenn.

How to Reach the Authors and MindTeam Solutions, Inc.

MindTeam Solutions, Inc. works with organizations that want engaged and productive employees and with leaders who want their staff to live a positive organizational culture. We begin our engagements by starting with a conversation and building relationships to learn whether, and how, we can best serve each other. You can reach us at:

MindTeam Solutions, Inc.
Up-to-date mailing address and phone numbers are at our website.
Website: www.MindTeamSolutions.com

 General business email: info@MindTeamSolutions.com

 Josh Silverstone: Josh@MindTeamSolutions.com

Sylvia Henderson: Sylvia@MindTeamSolutions.com

Connect with, follow, and subscribe to us at the social media links at our website.

More Books? Here's How to Get Them

Want more books to share with your leadership team and employees? Order more by scanning and emailing this order form to info@MindTeamSolutions.com, or online at http://mindteamsolutions.com/catalog.

Our USPS mailing address is MindTeam Solutions, Inc., 3570 Olney-Laytonsville Rd., #588, Olney, MD 20832, ATTN: Book Order.

Name:	Purchase Order #:
Company:	Date:
Billing Address:	
Shipping Address (if different from billing):	
Email:	Telephone:
Payment Info:	
Additional Notes?	

Quantity		Price $ (US Dollars)	Total $ (US Dollars)

For visionary talent leaders and C-suite teams who truly believe that their people are their greatest assets.

Made in the USA
Columbia, SC
07 November 2018